I very much appreciate Robert Scott's g
biblical approach to engaging with the
by his Muslim friends. His confidence i
gospel and his love and respect for others shine through. This book
will be very helpful to Christian students and others, as we seek to
engage Muslim students with the good news of Jesus Christ.
Natasha Kasprowicz, London Team Leader, UCCF

Robert Scott writes with a clear head and winning affection for
his Muslim friends. Instead of giving glib, pre-packaged
responses, he shows how the very shape of the gospel answers
Muslim objections to it – and thus he models how attractive the
Triune God of love is . . . very helpful.
Michael Reeves, Head of Theology, UCCF

Robert Scott is one of the brightest and most faithful young
ministers called to serve the church of Christ today. Here he
gives us a very well-written book with which to answer our dear
Muslim friends' sincere questions about the biblical faith. His
answers are penetrating, faithful and practical, with biblical and
historical understanding of the glorious gospel of our King Jesus
Christ. He demonstrates a high degree of Christian dignity and
a heart full of love for Muslim people around the globe.

I highly recommend this excellent work which will help
Muslims and Christians everywhere to have a better
understanding of their respective beliefs and each other. This
important work arrives at a critical moment for building bridges
with our Muslim friends. May the Lord use it for his glory and
honour among the nations.
Anees Zaka, Founder and Author of 'Meetings for Better Understanding'
concept, and Founder and President of Church Without Walls and the
Biblical Institute for Islamic Studies, both in Philadelphia

'Dear Abdullah'

ivp

Robert Scott

'Dear Abdullah'

Eight questions Muslim people ask about Christianity

INTER-VARSITY PRESS
Norton Street, Nottingham NG7 3HR, England
Email: ivp@ivpbooks.com
Website: www.ivpbooks.com

British Library Cataloguing in Publication Data
A catalogue record for this book is available from the British Library.

ISBN: 978–1–84474–528–9

Set in Dante 12/15pt
Typeset in Great Britain by CRB Associates, Potterhanworth, Lincolnshire
Printed in Great Britain by Ashford Colour Press Ltd, Gosport, Hampshire

*Inter-Varsity Press publishes Christian books that are true to the Bible and that
communicate the gospel, develop discipleship and strengthen the church for its
mission in the world.*

*Inter-Varsity Press is closely linked with the Universities and Colleges Christian
Fellowship, a student movement connecting Christian Unions in universities and
colleges throughout Great Britain, and a member movement of the International
Fellowship of Evangelical Students. Website: www.uccf.org.uk*

Contents

Acknowledgments

In rough chronological order of this book's genesis, I am very, very grateful to:

Muslim friends who have asked me many questions about Christianity and caused me to see the depth of riches in the Lord Jesus as I searched the Scriptures for answers to their queries; Anees for his model of Meetings for Better Understanding and help in setting them up, both in person and through his book, *Muslims and Christians at the Table* (co-authored with Bruce McDowell, Presbyterian & Reformed, 1999); Andrew's off-the-cuff suggestion that I should write up my MBU talks; my church's leadership team for giving me the time to do the writing; Lewis for unwittingly giving me the book's title from a conversation years ago; Iftikhar for his ongoing love and guidance in a gentle approach to talking about Jesus with Muslim friends; Martin and Steve for their wisdom and helpful ideas; Anne-Laure, Danielle, Joe and Marcus for being faithful students and helpful sounding boards; anonymous reviewers pointing me in useful directions and making me clearer; Kate and Mollie as editors (and correctors!) and driving the book forwards.

I am thankful to my family, for those before me whose sincere faith led to mine, and for those around me whose lives make me smile and keep me humble. And to my church family, who have shared their lives and the gospel with us.

And finally, to the One who holds me in his hands, whose hands were pierced for me and whose hands will wipe away all tears, I thank the Lord Jesus who became poor that I might become rich.

Foreword

Since the terrorist attacks in New York and Washington DC in September 2001, a huge amount of literature has been produced focusing on Islam and Christian-Muslim relations, designed to address the need both in the church and in the broader West to understand what motivates Muslims and to help people to respond in appropriate ways.

Rob Scott's book addresses part of that vast audience. It is intended especially for Christians who have a particular calling to engage with Muslims, but also for other Christians who simply seek to understand what has been going on in the world in connection with Islam over the last decade.

This book meets the accessibility test in three key ways. First, it focuses upon real questions posed by real Muslims to real Christians on a regular basis. Second, it provides answers that effectively equip Christians to engage with Muslims in diverse contexts. Third, it uses a style of language which is easily comprehensible for those with little background in the study of Islam.

On this basis, 'Dear Abdullah' deserves wide distribution among Christians as they interact with their Muslim friends, and it is a welcome addition to the literature on Islam and Christian-Muslim relations.

Peter Riddell
Professorial Dean, Centre for the Study of Islam and Other Faiths,
Melbourne School of Theology
Formerly Professor of Islamic Studies at London School of Theology

Introduction:
Questions, objections and confusion

Bad questions?

I was enjoying tucking into my rice and curry with Abdullah.[1] It was a little bland for my liking, but our friends at the mosque were probably thinking of me and the other Christians who were their guests. Abdullah had been in the United Kingdom for most of his life and was feeling a bit frustrated – many of his friends seemed to lack any sense of adventure. Their big-little world consisted of family, neighbourhood, mosque and not much else. He enjoyed getting out of London and hiking and so we shared different stories of getting cold and wet while walking in Wales.

Abdullah was sitting with me because he wanted to follow up something I had said in my talk earlier. Another Muslim friend and I had just shared a platform to explain to a group of Muslim and Christian people what it was like to live out our respective religions in our daily lives. It was part of a series of 'meetings for better understanding'. My talk had stuck to the Christian perspective, rather than critiquing the Islamic point of view, just as the Muslim speaker had stuck to Islam and didn't criticize Christianity. This, I suspect, had frustrated Yusuf, Abdullah's friend.

Just as Abdullah was getting beyond Wales and on to his particular question, Yusuf sat down and without any introduction asked, 'Do you think Jesus is a prophet? Or do you think he's the Son of God?' Before I had time to reply, he followed up with 'If he's God's Son, did God have sex with Mary? If he's divine, don't you follow two gods? And if he *is* divine, then how come Jesus got hungry and thirsty and was tired and was born in the first place?'

I began to answer Yusuf's questions, but after a minute or so Abdullah interrupted. This time it wasn't about religion: 'Would you like some more rice, Robert?'

As we stood in the rice queue, Abdullah had a knowing smile on his face, and so I thanked him for rescuing me from what was probably going to be a fruitless conversation.

Yusuf's questions are not bad questions. They are common questions put to Christian people, and have been asked since the earliest centuries of Islam. They do need to be answered by followers of Jesus the Messiah – who is both Prophet and Son of God, fully human and fully divine. Indeed such questions from my Muslim friends have helped me to grow in my faith as they have taken me back to the holy Scriptures to find answers. However, the tone used by Yusuf and others like him can often leave a lot to be desired. Such a questioner rarely seems interested in the answers.

Therefore, rather than be tied down by these kinds of ongoing questions, maybe a different response is in order, such as 'I'll reply to you if you can tell me whether the Qur'an is created or eternal'. (Jesus the Messiah used this sort of approach when the religious people of his day tried to trap him; see for example Matthew 21:23–27.) It isn't a knock-down irrefutable response and has been discussed by Muslim scholars since at least the eighth century,[2] but the question does allow you to gauge the person's sincerity: are they an Abdullah or a Yusuf?

This book is written for the Abdullahs, the men and women who share our communities, our lectures and halls of residences, our offices and blocks of flats. These are the people of peace whom Jesus the Messiah told his disciples to look for (see Luke 10:5–7 in the New Testament or *Injil*[3]) – such as the lawyer in Mark 10:28–34, Nicodemus in John 3:1–15, the Samaritan woman in John 4:1–40 and the man born blind in John 9. These are people who are genuinely interested in understanding who the Christ of this Christian message really is. This book begins to address their real questions, objections and confusion concerning our message. Therefore I hope it can be given to such Muslim friends. However, it's also written for Christians, so that they can answer these questions in as gentle and honest a way as possible.

Central objections

As most people know, Islam has five 'pillars' or basic practices: a Muslim must make the confession of faith that 'There is no God but God and Muhammad is his prophet', pray five times a day, give alms, fast during Ramadan and go on pilgrimage to Mecca. It also has six or so central beliefs: in the oneness of God, his angels, his messengers/prophets, his revealed books, the Day of Judgment and God's divine sovereign will.[4] Along with these, there are probably four key theological objections which most Muslim people have to the Christian message:[5]

1. Jesus did not die on a cross.
2. Jesus is neither the Son of God nor divine.
3. The Trinity is wrong.
4. The Bible is corrupted.

I cannot think of a Muslim friend who has not raised at least one of these objections with me at some point in our friendship. These objections seem common to most Muslim people because they can be gleaned from the Qur'an or the teachings of Muhammad or later Islamic scholars. In many ways, these objections go to the heart of the Christian message. Therefore it's right that we should discuss them, as this book does in chapters 3, 4, 5 and 7.

Wider responses

I am also keen to cover issues that go beyond these four objections. This is because, first, my experience of meetings for better understanding has shown that it can be really helpful to offer simple explanations of other areas of the Christian faith (such as who God is, what Christians do each day and how this fits with Western culture). This can give our Muslim friends a deeper appreciation of what it means to follow Jesus Christ. Talking about these topics has also led them to ask genuine questions rather than repeat the more usual 'four objections'. Therefore, chapters 1, 2 and 6 will address these areas specifically. The book properly begins in the next chapter concerning who God is. This is because every religious discussion must start with the Greater Reality from which its religion springs and whom its followers are to know, live for and promote.

Second, even if we were to concentrate on these four objections, any response involves an explanation of other Christian doctrines. Many people in our culture and within some churches hate the term 'doctrine'. But it isn't a dirty word and it doesn't mean forcing people to believe what is right and wrong. Doctrine simply means teaching, and all Christians believe certain teachings about the faith.[6] Just as Richard Dawkins' doctrine of science affects his understanding of nature, humanity and religion, so everybody's individual beliefs affect other convictions they have (although these convictions may not always be consistent with one another!).

Therefore any explanation of why Jesus the Messiah died and rose again relates to the biblical doctrine of sin. Or any description of God as three persons touches on our understanding of humans as personal and relational beings. As Christians we want to show these linkages in order to be faithful to the Christian message. These linkages also add weight and coherence to our message.

Third, the five pillars and six beliefs can lead some Muslim people to have a respect for their God but not to think that he is involved in their everyday lives. As a result, everyday life is left as a 'space' which needs to be dealt with by individual Muslim people themselves, often by practising what is known as 'folk Islam'.[7]

This space is where questions of fear, sickness, loneliness, guilt, revenge, shame, powerlessness, longing, meaninglessness and crisis prevail. It is also where more mystical beliefs can dominate, where people don't so much confess the name of God as use it magically for protection, where they venerate angels and prophets, use holy books as charms, think that almsgiving will ward off the 'evil eye', and much more. For Muslim friends with these concerns, the issue of getting information and answering objections is not always top of their agenda. Rather, these men and women are searching for the power and protection that only Jesus the Messiah can bring. Therefore, in concluding some of the chapters, I try to apply the Bible's teaching to some of the everyday needs of our Muslim friends.

Each chapter also ends with several key points and a few questions. The key points are an attempt to summarize the argument of that chapter. I say 'attempt' because summaries of anything can be difficult, and summaries of religious doctrine even more so. There is always more that can be said and more nuances that can be included.

In the fourth season of the popular drama series *The West Wing*, President Josiah Bartlet takes part in a TV debate with the other presidential candidate, Governor Robert Ritchie. Bartlet pounces on his opponent's desire to answer every question with a sound bite or just ten words: 'Ten-word answers can kill you in a political campaign. They're the tip of the sword. My question is, "What are the *next* ten words of your answer?" . . . There aren't very many un-nuanced moments in leading a country that's way too big for ten words.'

Just as it's hard to lead a country with ten words or sound bites, so it's hard to convey the breadth and depth of the wonders of our great God in just a few key points. So please don't think that the key points are the whole answer, but hopefully they are something of a truthful answer.

The questions at the end of each chapter are for two kinds of people. The first set is for followers of Jesus who want to think these things through in a bit more depth, designed to help them be more able to present these truths to their Muslim friends. The second set is for those Muslim friends, to help them see some of the implications of Christianity's claims as well as the contrast with Islam. I hope that both kinds of people are able to apply to their lives the truths they find in each chapter. After all, unapplied knowledge is a bit of a contradiction.

A word more on method

Our postmodern Western culture is suspicious of people who make truth claims. My Muslim friends sometimes echo such sentiments with replies like 'That's just your interpretation!' whenever we look at a Bible passage together.

This kind of challenge should make us humble bearers of truth, rather than lead us to deny truth claims altogether or be arrogantly coercive. The cries of the 'postmoderns' and our Muslim friends concerning interpretation should also be heard, but not at the expense of accepting all interpretations as equally valid and true. Rather, our interpretations should be justified and consistent. Also, the frameworks which led to these interpretations should be open for all to see. This transparency helps others to better evaluate our truth claims and guards us against accusations of impure motives and hidden agendas. This is partly why, in a doctors' journal like the *British Medical Journal*, each article is followed by a paragraph on the author's 'competing interests', so that readers can better evaluate the truth in the research.

So here is a little of my background: I am a Christian who grew up in a Christian family in south-east England. I studied social anthropology at university and worked in Bangladesh shortly afterwards. I am married and have three children. Prior to working for an evangelical Anglican church, I worked for the World Health Organization.

I studied theology at an Anglican college. I heartily agree with the orthodox Christian creeds of the first five centuries AD, with much of the Reformation confessions of faith dating from the sixteenth and seventeenth centuries, and with evangelical doctrinal bases and statements on the Bible made in the twentieth century.[8] Since university, I have been ever more convinced that the holy Bible is God's Word (more about this in chapter 7!) and that God works in people as his Word is read and proclaimed. When understood rightly, in its literary and historical context, I am convinced that it is literally true and authoritative in all matters of faith and conduct.

Therefore I try to answer each objection or question addressed in the following chapters from the Bible, while also drawing on insights from orthodox followers of Jesus who have gone before me. Such a stance can shock some people, as I stand by what the Bible teaches on marriage or hell. It can shock my Muslim friends when I stand by what the Bible teaches on the nature of God or the work of Jesus Christ. However, the Bible's teachings also convince me that all people everywhere are made in God's image, even those who disagree with me, and they are worthy of great dignity, care and love.

Additionally, the Bible convinces me that everyone everywhere has marred this image and is estranged from God. This means that all people, including atheist and Muslim people, need to be restored and reconciled through the love of the Lord Jesus Christ. This love is only truly revealed in the holy Bible and so I want to present it here.

As I wrote this book, I tried to stay true to the holy Bible as well as to remember the humanity of my readers, whatever their backgrounds. I also shied away from using the Qur'an too much because it isn't 'my' book. I am often frustrated by Muslim friends who try to twist the Bible to fit their agenda. I have tried not to do the same with the Qur'an. I have referred to the Qur'an to show the possible origin of a particular objection to Christianity, or in order to raise a question in Muslim people's minds. I have tried not to belittle Islam, but to give an answer with 'gentleness and respect' wherever I can (1 Peter 3:15–16). I suspect that some readers, whether Christian or Muslim or others, will think that my answers are too black and white in places, or too nuanced in others, or just plain wrong. However, I hope they will bear with this and be like the good Bereans, who 'examined the Scriptures . . . to see if what [the Christians] said was true' (Acts 17:10–15).

A word more on the Qur'an

Just as I would encourage every reader to look up the Bible passages I refer to, not least to check that I am not making things up, so I would encourage readers to check the Qur'anic references too. If you don't have a Qur'an, you could borrow one from a Muslim friend or maybe ask them to suggest a good place to buy one. Many of the bigger mosques are happy to give them away free or have an Islamic bookshop near to them. The most popular English translation is by Abdullah Yusuf Ali and is the one generally quoted in this book. Muhammad Marmaduke Pickthall is an honest translator with some helpful historical background to the Qur'an usually included (and he has a great name too!). M. A. S. Abdel Haleem, the Professor of Islamic Studies at the School of Oriental and African Studies in London, has published a new translation in the Oxford World's Classics series which is usually pretty readable.

Many Qur'ans come with footnotes or appendices to explain verses. You can often understand the translator's perspectives and biases from these. Therefore these are worth looking at to gain a feel for the translator.

As you probably know, the Qur'an is not put together in the same way as the Bible. The Qur'an is not arranged in chronological or thematic order. Chapters which Muhammad preached in Mecca often follow chapters that he preached in Medina, although he lived in Mecca prior to Medina. Therefore it can be hard to find your way around the Qur'an and to understand it. Most Qur'ans, however, have an index which can help you pull together various verses on a particular topic.

That said, much of the interpretation for the Qur'an comes from outside the Qur'an. The key to interpretation often lies in Muhammad's own life, as recorded in the Hadith. Hadith collections are also available in Islamic bookshops, but there are very many of these and so it is probably best to start with the Qur'an.

Seeking better understanding and looking to a better day post-7/7

Over the last five or six years, my church has been involved in around fifteen meetings for better understanding. One of these events took place on the Sunday after the 7/7 bombings in London. We thought that the meeting might not happen or that it would lead to angry exchanges. Instead, we stood together in silence to remember the dead at Aldgate, King's Cross and Holborn, as well as victims of war in Iraq and Afghanistan. Instead, we had the opportunity to show our commonalities and differences as we lived as Muslims and Christians in London. Instead, I had the opportunity to help a dozen Abdullahs to see that God, as revealed in the holy Bible, is interested in our everyday lives and is concerned for us to be with him in his new heavens and new earth. This is the place which Surah 14:48 seems to look forward to:

> One day the Earth will be changed to a different Earth, and so will be the Heavens.
> (Yusuf Ali's translation, as are all subsequent quotations from the Qur'an unless stated otherwise)

This new creation is one where all the anger, destruction and mess of this life have been removed. It is where Jesus the Messiah opens the gates for us to enter. It is where those who follow Jesus will fully experience the title 'friend of God' (khalilullah in Arabic), which the prophet and patriarch Abraham was given. This book is written in the hope that a Muslim friend like Abdullah (which means 'Slave of God') might one day become a khalilullah. As the Scriptures make clear, anyone can be brought out of slavery and become a friend of God, by believing in the promises God made to Abraham – promises fulfilled by Jesus the Messiah.[9]

1. How can we know an incomprehensible God?

Allahu akbar! The God of the Bible is great!

God seems greatly incomprehensible

'Robert, you have just said that "God is love". You have said that this love is shared with people. I know how to love my wife, but I cannot know what the love of almighty Allah is like. His love is so far above ours.'

Prior to meeting Abdullah and Yusuf, we had held a similar meeting for better understanding in that same mosque. The topic this time was our respective conceptions of God. I mentioned the apostle John's words that 'God is love' (1 John 4:8). In the Questions and Answers session afterwards, the sheikh sitting beside me responded to this with the words of the paragraph above. He carried on: 'Love is a human concept and we cannot draw analogies from human love to God's love. We cannot understand God as love in any way.'

I had heard similar views before. It seems a fairly orthodox Muslim position – we are creatures and cannot understand our Creator. It's a statement of humility, but it's also a statement of profound despair.

If human words and concepts have no link with God in any way, we can know nothing about God. All we have are human words, and these creaturely words cannot convey understanding about God. We are left in our creatureliness. We are in the dark about God. There is an unbridgeable chasm between us and any knowledge of God. We can neither know about his mercy nor personally experience it because it cannot be communicated to mere creatures like us.

This really does leave many of my Muslim friends with a God they cannot comprehend or even truly describe to others. This problem seems to be understood by some Muslim speakers. More than once, I have visited university Islamic societies to listen to talks on 'The God of Islam'. But they turned out to be talks on 'Islam as the religion of peace' or 'How to submit to God' rather than attempts to describe or explain the Greater Reality which people are supposed to follow.

As followers of Jesus the Messiah, we need not be silent on who God is. We can give comforting content to the claim that 'God is great'. This is because God humbled himself to communicate to us in human language, through using created concepts and ultimately by coming to live within his creation.

God is . . .

The holy Bible speaks of God in many different ways. For example, God is called a 'Rock' (Psalm 19:14). Does this mean that he is literally a rock? No, as this would mean a one-to-one correspondence between the word 'Rock' and what it is referring to. Could it mean that God is actually a sponge? No, as this would mean there is *no* link between the word 'Rock' and what it is trying to convey about God.

Instead, the description of God as a Rock is a metaphor or analogy. It emphasizes the security and safety which God provides for his people, just as a rock does if you build on it. God uses human words and things in creation to reveal himself to us. So God is also a shepherd guiding and guarding his people (Psalm 23), a bird caring for her young (Psalm 17:8), a mighty warrior (Exodus 15:1–21), a father (Isaiah 64:8), a husband (Hosea 2:16) and a lion (Jeremiah 49:19), to name but a few analogies.

The Bible also tells us about God's attributes or characteristics. For example, God is eternal (Deuteronomy 33:27; Romans 1:20), unchangeable (Numbers 23:19; Malachi 3:6), omnipresent (Psalm 139:7–12), omnipotent (Jeremiah 32:17; Revelation 4:11) and so on.

Sometimes the Scriptures also tell us that God *is* something, in his essence or essential nature. For instance, after living with Jesus the Messiah and getting to know him personally, the apostle John was able to write, under God's inspiration, that God *is* light and God *is* love (1 John 1:5; 4:8). These two concepts are profound in their implications. For example, 'God is light' means that he is pure, perfect and holy. Therefore, we as impure, darkened and sinful creatures can never be in his presence. Light banishes darkness. Does this mean that God will banish people too? Fortunately, the answer is found in 'God is love'. God in himself, and from all eternity, has always been love. This love flows out to the world, enabling people to know him and come near to him.

However, rather than concentrate on these concepts or attributes or analogies, this chapter is going to focus elsewhere. Rather than think about *what* God or divinity is, we are going to look at *who* God is. Throughout God's Word, we are given clear and consistent ways of characterizing God or explaining who he is. We see this as the Bible unfolds its narrative and God relates to his world.

God is Creator and Ruler

The first page of the Bible introduces us to God:

> In the beginning God created the heavens and the earth.
> Now the earth was formless and empty, darkness was over the
> surface of the deep, and the Spirit of God was hovering over
> the face of the waters.
>
> And God said, 'Let there be light,' and there was light. God
> saw that the light was good.
> (*Taurat*, Genesis 1:1–4)[1]

Why begin here? First, it is the beginning of the Bible and how
God introduces himself to us. Therefore it isn't a bad place
to start.

Second, it is a common concept that we share with our
Muslim friends. They believe in a Creator too. (The fact that
many Muslim apologists are debating with atheists on
creation and design makes this point.) While the Creator has
different connotations in the Qur'an, it is something of a
shared basis from which we can start to talk about God. This
seems to be the approach which the apostle Paul took in
Athens as he revealed 'the unknown God' to his audience
(Acts 17:16–34).

Third, and probably most importantly, this may be the
best approach when reading the Bible with people who don't
know much about its content, whether atheist postmoderns
or devout Muslims. Of course we want to proclaim Jesus as
Lord and Saviour, but if people don't know the context into
which he proclaims himself as Lord and Saviour then he
can sound irrelevant to our atheist friends or blasphemous
to our Muslim friends. Therefore, it's important not only to
listen to what the holy Scriptures say about who God is, but
to do so in such a way that we understand the Bible's story

from beginning to end and how God's plans are revealed progressively.

Back to Genesis. As you may know, the rest of the first chapter of the Bible carries on the theme of creation. God simply speaks and things come into existence, from the sun and moon to centipedes and mooses, from mountains and waters to men and women. God's word is powerful and effective.

The prophet Moses wrote Genesis 1 under God's inspiration. (While there is some debate about the authorship of the first five books of the Bible, as there is with other ancient texts, I see no reason to disagree with Jesus or with the majority of Christians over time and space who have regarded these books as written by Moses.[2]) Moses wanted all people everywhere to realize that the God of the Bible is the Creator. He alone made everything.

These truths are echoed in the words of a contemporary song:

> Creation sings the Father's song;
> He calls the sun to wake the dawn
> And run the course of day
> Till evening falls in crimson rays.
> His fingerprints in flakes of snow,
> His breath upon this spinning globe,
> He charts the eagle's flight;
> Commands the newborn baby's cry.
> (Extract taken from the song 'Creation Sings the Father's Song' by Kristyn Getty, Keith Getty and Stuart Townend, copyright © 2008 Thankyou Music[3])

And in old songs, which the Bible itself records, like those of King David:

The earth is the LORD's,[4] and everything in it,
    the world, and all who live in it;
for he founded it upon the seas
    and established it upon the waters.
(*Zabur*, Psalm 24:1–2)

These words imply that God is the Creator. God made every-thing, which means he owns everything and rules over it. The earth is the LORD's because he established it.

I enjoy DIY. Sad, but true. Maybe it's the sense of achieve-ment at making bookshelves that don't collapse (a job I can tick off!). Maybe it's a sense of fulfilling the creation mandate through making a shoe rack. That said, perhaps most signifi-cantly, the shelves and rack I have cobbled together are *mine*. Both are for their creator's own use, not for anyone else's. I might allow other people to put their books on my shelves or their shoes on my rack, but that's for me to decide because I own the shelves and the rack. This is the same for God, albeit on a much larger scale!

If God owns everything because he made it, this also means that he is our world's rightful ruler. This is a key lesson which God teaches throughout his holy Scriptures. He alone is Creator and Ruler, not the gods of Canaan or Pharaoh or the imperial powers of Assyria and Babylon.[5] It is a theme which begins the Bible and grows through time as more and more of Israel's prophets call people to acknowledge that the LORD is God and there is no other.

This is why the Bible is full of commands for us to love the LORD our God with all our heart, soul, strength and mind (for example, Deuteronomy 6:5). There is no other who should have our hearts and our devotion. God as Creator-Owner-Ruler tells us that we are not autonomous. I cannot do what I like with my life, my body, my time, MySpace or anything else which I think is mine. I am created and therefore owned and ruled by my Creator. This has much to say to our Western culture and its obsession with independence, not to mention how we treat other people whom God has made.

God is the personal Covenant-Maker . . .

. . . in an overarching narrative
God is initially described as the Creator and Ruler. This is a theme which is threaded throughout the Bible's narrative. However, as with all good narratives the main character is given greater depth and colour as time goes on. The Bible's narrative achieves this as it lays out God's actions in his world and how he means to restore it.

For some people the idea that the Scriptures have an overarching storyline is new, but we can see this by very briefly comparing its first and last chapters. The first three chapters of the Bible in Genesis and the last two chapters of the Bible in Revelation pick up the same kind of themes and ideas:

Genesis 2 Blessings	Genesis 3 Curses	Revelation 21 – 22 Amazing blessings
Intimate and good relationship with God (verses 7–18; see also 3:8)	Broken relationship with God (verses 10–13)	God will be with his people (21:3–4)
Harmonious relationship with each other (verses 22–24)	Broken relationship with each other (verses 6–7, 12, 16)	No crying or pain (21:4); healed nations (22:2); no curse (22:3)
In God's land (verses 8–15)	Out of the land (verses 23–24)	In God's city (21:1–3, 22–27)

Genesis 2 Blessings	Genesis 3 Curses	Revelation 21 – 22 Amazing blessings
Pleasant work under God (verse 15)	Pain and suffering (verses 16–19)	No pain or suffering, serving God perfectly (21:4; 22:3)
Eternal life (see also 3:22)	Death (verses 19, 22)	Receive life, no curse of death (21:6; 22:3)

What was lost by Adam and Eve in Genesis 3 is restored in Revelation 21 – 22. Having been punished by God and thrown out of his paradise, God's people are blessed and are back in his paradise by the end. The rest of the Bible between these brackets or bookends explains how we move from a fallen creation to the new creation.

Within this narrative we see God repeatedly relating to people in similar ways. This in itself shows that he is personal and not a mere individual. A person is someone in relationship with others. Personhood is about going out from yourself and being relational. An individual is simply a being without reference to anyone else. It is something that can be divided off. But how does God personally relate to people?

He does it through a 'covenant'. This is an agreement between God and people in which God commits himself to people, promising blessings to them, and describes the conditions of their relationship with him.

It's like a marriage. This is an agreement between one man and one woman to commit publicly to one another, through thick and thin, in sickness and in health, in an exclusive relationship. Others are witnesses to the agreement and there may be a certificate to verify it. Interestingly, God often describes the relationship with his people as a marriage.[6] Holy

Scripture acts as both the marriage certificate and the photo album. It witnesses to what God says and does and how his people respond.

. . . personally relating to people

In order to make a covenant, God needed to appoint a mediator. This was someone who could act on behalf of the people. So God appointed Adam (Hosea 6:7), Noah (Genesis 9:9), Abraham (Genesis 17:3–7), Moses (Exodus 24:7) and David (2 Samuel 23:5; see also 2 Samuel 7:1–17). These were people of great faith – the leaders of God's people in their day. The Qur'an seems to recognize something of their unique status as covenant mediators in Surah 33:7.

God related to these people personally and intimately. He walked with Adam in the cool of the garden (Genesis 3:8). He appeared to Abraham and ate with him (Genesis 18:1–33). He declared his glory to Moses on Mount Sinai and allowed him access to his throne room (Exodus 24; 34:1–9). He spoke with David and fought for him (2 Samuel 5:23–25; see also 2 Kings 6:17).

From this we can see that it is not the New Testament or the apostle Paul or the early church or the emperor Constantine who fabricated the idea that the Creator and Ruler of the world came to be with his people. When talking about Jesus, my Muslim friends have often accused one of these suspects of bringing God to earth. They often argue that it's an idea foreign to the God of the Old Testament. However, this is not the case. The Creator God with whom the Bible begins comes near to his creatures.

. . . amid promised blessings and human failings

This God promised his people life, protection, land, a future as a great nation and a kingdom of peace. He also promised curses and punishment for those who rejected the covenant and worshipped other gods. This can be described as spiritual adultery. Just as it's wrong for me to go after other women and dishonour my wife and our marriage covenant, so it's wrong for God's people to turn from him and chase after other gods.

Unfortunately, Bible history shows that people are incapable of loving God with all of their hearts (as we know of ourselves, if we're honest). Just as Adam and Eve broke up the first covenant by disobeying God, preferring to believe Satan and call God a liar, so did people ever after. Indeed, shortly after Adam and Eve, God told Noah that every inclination of the thoughts of our hearts is only evil all of the time (Genesis 6:5). Hundreds of years later, the prophet Jeremiah echoed God's verdict:

> The heart is deceitful above all things
>> and beyond cure.
>> Who can understand it?
> (Prophet Jeremiah 17:9)

Even children are not exempt from this. David, the prophet and king, tells us in Psalm 51 that he was full of sin from the beginning of his life, even within the womb. Or as the wise King Solomon succinctly put it:

> Folly is bound up in the heart of a child.
> (Proverbs 22:15)

In view of this, it is astonishing that God promised a new covenant which would sort out people's hearts. God promised to put his law within people and put it on their hearts (Jeremiah 31:31–37). The prophet Ezekiel explains these words further as he tells us that God will rescue people from their sin, clean up their hearts and put a new spirit, his Spirit, within them (Ezekiel 36:24–27). (Sin's seriousness and its consequences are described in a little more detail in chapter 3.)

And the prophet Isaiah gives us the wonderful promise that God will make an everlasting covenant with his people (Isaiah 61:8). This is an eternal, better covenant which brings peace with God. It ends our guilt and shame before God. It ends war between people. It brings the final defeat of death and evil. Isaiah's words from God in chapter 40 onwards explain these marvellous truths. Those chapters also declare that God will reveal his deity through a suffering servant and by coming to live with humble men and women (for example, Isaiah 57:15; we will see more in chapters 3, 4 and 5 of this book).

Therefore it is no surprise when John the Baptist tells us that Jesus the Messiah will baptize people not with water but with the Holy Spirit, as Jeremiah and Ezekiel promised (John 1:29–34). It is no surprise that Jesus the Messiah tells us that his death and resurrection are the means of a new and better covenant which will last forever (Luke 22:20; Hebrews 8 – 10), as Isaiah told us. And just as God walked with the people of his previous covenants, so it is no surprise that God lives with the humble people of his new and better covenant, as Isaiah promised.

Comfort from this great God

The eternal Word of God, Jesus the Messiah, came to live with ordinary human beings on earth in order to reveal God more fully and more truly (John 1:14–18). His coming was the culmination of God's progressive revelation of himself, which began in Genesis 1. In Jesus the Messiah we see what God is like: he is full of grace and truth. This grace means that weak, sinful, shameful, dark-hearted people like us can be forgiven and brought near to our awesome Creator and Ruler. This truth means that the shadowy outlines of the old covenant are fulfilled and we can know God as he truly is. He is the great God of the Bible.

This can be a mind-bending truth for my orthodox Muslim friends who appear to have no personal knowledge of their remote Creator. It sounds too good to be true. This is why we must help such friends to see that the Bible's Creator has always been personal and covenant-making. This is why we must begin at the story's beginning and show how Jesus the Messiah fulfils all the promises which the Old Testament talks about.

It can also seem almost incredible for our less orthodox friends who feel at the mercy of angels and demons and are fearful for the future. The orthodox God, who is removed from their world, seems to leave space for other powers to operate in the lives of Muslim men and women. An impersonal God cannot be concerned for what happens to *me* each day. Therefore I need magic for protection, or a particular spiritual leader to give me insight and help.

This is what makes Jesus the Messiah so attractive. Let us rejoice in the Jesus who meets our and our friends' deepest needs. Through Jesus the Messiah we can know God personally. We can know that God is for us and that nothing can separate us from his love. Neither angels nor demons, neither present or future, no power, nothing in all creation can separate us from God or his love or his eternal covenant – which anyone can have through Jesus the Messiah (Romans 8:28–39). Therefore I don't need to be anxious today, tomorrow or even about what will happen to me beyond death. I have a loving God who cares for me (Matthew 6:25–34). How this should impact our everyday living and not simply remain a comforting truth is dealt with in the next chapter.

When the apostle Paul presented the citizens of Athens with the truth about the 'unknown god' that they worshipped, some people sneered and mocked him. That has sometimes been my experience when I have talked about these truths with Muslim people. However, as was the case with Paul, others wanted to hear more about this subject. Why not pray for both an opportunity to talk about these things with your Muslim friends and for them to want to hear about it again? It seems that most Muslim people need to listen to this kind of teaching many times before the Holy Spirit writes it upon their hearts.

Also, even at Islam's beginning, there were those who turned to follow this one, true God, as some did in Athens (Acts 17:32–34). For example, one of the oldest records of Muhammad's life and work says:

> 'Ubaydullah went on searching [for truth] until Islam came; then he migrated with the Muslims to Abyssinia taking with him his wife who was a Muslim, Umm Ḥabība, d. Abū Sufyān. When he arrived there he adopted Christianity, parted from Islam, and died a Christian in Abyssinia. Muhammad b. Ja'far b. al-Zubayr told me that when he had become a Christian 'Ubaydullah as he passed the prophet's companions who were there used to say: 'We see clearly, but your eyes are only half open,' i.e. 'We see, but you are only trying to see and cannot see yet.' He used the word *ṣa'ṣa'* because when a puppy tries to open its eyes to see, it only half sees. The other word *faqqaha* means to open the eyes.[7]

'Ubaydullah had his eyes opened to see the truth about God. My prayer is that our Muslim friends will have their eyes opened too so that they can personally know our great God and receive his rock-like security.

Key points

- God is great and knowable because he is the Creator, Ruler and personal Covenant-Maker.
- God has always made promises to his people and made ways to be with them.
- These promises are ultimately fulfilled in the Lord Jesus who brings in the last covenant and assures us of God's ongoing and eternal security.

Some questions

For followers of Jesus the Messiah

- Is it new for you to see that God is the personal Covenant-Maker?
- How does this truth bring both a challenge and comfort from God?
- How confident would you be about reading Genesis with a Muslim friend to help him or her to see the Bible's narrative?

For Muslim friends

- How is God as Creator and Ruler similar or different to what you know of him?
- What do you think of the idea that God makes promises or covenants with people?
- How do you think that God relates to his world?

2. Don't Christians only do Sundays?

Living each day for God

One-day-a-week Christianity?

I recently visited some Bengali friends. Hasan the father proudly said, 'I pray five times a day in my mosque, while you pray only once on a Sunday.' Some Muslim friends have gone further and said that Christianity is one-dimensional and only concerned with life after death. Therefore it isn't practised in everyday life.

Unfortunately, there is some truth to these misconceptions. Muslim people sometimes see Christians being Christian only on a Sunday morning. Sometimes they hear us talking only about eternal salvation (as important as this is!). However, in response to this, we must not simply talk about living transformed lives every day of the week (as important as this is!) but also tell them *why* we live these lives.

There is an old tale about a humble farmer who had grown some carrots (I guess it could be any root vegetable, but carrots it is). He loved the king of his country very much and so travelled to the royal palace to give him some of his harvest. While courtiers sniggered at the sight of a poor farmer presenting carrots to the rich and powerful sovereign, the king himself was grateful. He recognized that the farmer was being generous with his meagre resources. In response he gave the farmer an enormous field as a gift.

One of the courtiers saw this and did some quick mental maths: *Wow, a field for some carrots! If I give the king a bigger gift, just think what he'll give to me!* So the man went to the market and bought a fine stallion. It was a beautiful horse and cost him all his savings.

The next day, the courtier very proudly presented the horse to the king. The king said a polite 'Thank you' and then carried on with his business.

The courtier was a bit puzzled by this and waited for the king to say something more. After a few minutes the king looked up from his papers. 'Is there a problem?' he asked.

'Well, Your Majesty, I'm a little confused. Yesterday a poor farmer gave you some carrots and you gave him a huge field. Today I gave you a mighty stallion and you haven't said anything about it, let alone rewarded me for my generosity.'

'Yes,' said the king, 'that's because you weren't really giving me the horse. You were giving it to yourself. You gave me something in order to be rewarded yourself.'

It's a quaint illustration, but I hope that it helps to show that both the 'what' and the 'why' are important. As important as it is to live each day for God, we should be doing so for the right reasons. For example, Jesus' teaching in his Sermon on the Mount says that our 'acts of righteousness', whether they are giving to the needy or praying or fasting, should not just be done, but done in the right way (Matthew 6:1–18).

The 'why' of 24/7 Christianity
Unlike the courtier who wanted a reward and unlike those who do good to avoid punishment, Christians live out their

religion because God has already blessed them and not punished them. To explain this further we will look at the New Testament letter of 1 Peter (we could go to almost anywhere in the Bible, but 1 Peter gives us one of the most straightforward explanations).

Peter, the 'apostle' or ambassador of Christ, was writing to Christian people in Turkey. Turkey was one of the first places to hear the good news of Jesus the Messiah as it spread from Jerusalem around the Mediterranean, into Europe and North Africa. Peter calls these Christians

> a chosen people, a royal priesthood, a holy nation, a people
> belonging to God, that you may declare the praises of him
> who called you out of darkness into his wonderful light.
> Once you were not a people, but now you are the people of
> God; once you had not received mercy, but now you have
> received mercy.
> (*Injil*, 1 Peter 2:9–10)

'Chosen people', 'royal priesthood', 'holy nation', 'belonging to God' – these phrases show that Christians have a very special identity. Followers of Jesus the Messiah have been brought into his royal and divine family. But how has this happened?

Peter says that God did this by calling them out of darkness. Darkness here is a metaphor for sin, rejection of God and worshipping false gods. Christian people have been called out of this darkness through the mercy of the God who is light.

This mercy comes because

> Christ died for sins once for all, the righteous for the
> unrighteous, to bring you to God . . . [You are saved] by the

resurrection of Jesus Christ, who has gone into heaven and is
at God's right hand – with angels, authorities and powers in
submission to him.

(*Injil*, 1 Peter 3:18, 21–22)

Jesus the Messiah is the sinless one (1 Peter 2:22) who bore
our sins and took our punishment. His wounds enabled us to
come into the light, to the God who *is* light. Therefore we
don't live as Christians in order to enter God's family but
because we are already in it. We don't live as Christians in
order to receive God's mercy but rather because we have
already received it.

Jesus the Messiah's resurrection on the first Easter Sunday
also shows us that he has conquered evil. All angels, authorities and powers are subject to him. He has conquered death
and all the evil powers associated with darkness. Therefore
we live every day in his light and without fear of evil.

In the terms of the quaint tale about the courtier and the
farmer, we don't give our King a horse in order to be freed
from evil; we give our King a few carrots because he has
already freed us. We give him our lives out of thanks and a
desire to live in the right way as true representatives of his
family. This is a much better motivation for living a good life
than doing so in order to get something in return.

The 'what' of 24/7 Christianity

Now that God has made Jesus' followers his people, we are to
declare his wonderful nature, plans and promises to the world
– the kinds of things we looked at in the last chapter. As the
apostle Peter himself says,

you are a chosen people, a royal priesthood, a holy nation,
a people belonging to God, that you may declare the

praises of him who called you out of darkness into his
wonderful light.
(*Injil*, 1 Peter 2:9)

This proclaiming is not simply about what we say, but also
how we act. Peter goes on to describe various ways in which
our praise of God can be seen. These provide a taste of what
it's like to live as a Christian every day.

Abstaining from sin

Dear friends, I urge you, as aliens and strangers in the world,
to abstain from sinful desires, which war against your soul.
(*Injil*, 1 Peter 2:11)

If sin is rebelling against God and worshipping a god made in
our own image, it doesn't make sense for Christians to sin.
We are in God's family, so why would we want to rebel against
him, bringing shame on our family and not living in the family
likeness?

As I write, José Mourinho has left Inter Milan football club
to manage Real Madrid. When Real Madrid next play Inter
Milan in the Champions' League, who should Mourinho plan
his strategy for? While he was once the Inter Milan manager,
he isn't their boss any more. Therefore it doesn't make sense
for him to try to unpick Real Madrid's defensive system or
work out how he can shackle Cristiano Ronaldo and company.
Mourinho has been chosen to manage a new team. He should
be fighting against the opposition of his new team.

Protection from envy

In a similar way, as Christians we should be fighting against
sin because we are now on God's heavenly side. Therefore, as

God's chosen people, living in his heavenly light, we are to rid ourselves of sinful desires, such as

> all malice and all deceit, hypocrisy, envy, and slander of
> every kind.
> (*Injil*, 1 Peter 2:1)

Suppose a colleague at work is promoted and I am overlooked. How should I react to this?

God's Word tells me to rid myself of any envy that I might feel towards my colleague. Such envy isn't appropriate for a follower of Jesus Christ. One obvious reason is that I have absolutely no basis for envy because I have enormous riches and wonderful status already through Jesus. Why envy someone for their money or status – neither of which lasts – when I have been brought into God's family and can look forward to an eternity in paradise?

Envy can work in other ways too. What if I was promoted and my colleague was overlooked? He might well be envious of me. In some cultures this envy can become a personification of evil. Or it can create an 'evil eye' which brings curses on the person who has gained something. The classical tale *A Thousand and One Arabian Nights* is full of such supernatural and magical fears, as are some of the homes near me in East London.

Some years ago Ruhana told us how she had grown coriander for her husband's curry house. The first year it had grown very well and had kept his restaurant in coriander for months. The next year, as it started to grow, a neighbour came over and commented on how good it looked. After a few weeks Ruhana's coriander died. To her mind this was because of her neighbour. She felt that her neighbour had been envious of the coriander and had an 'evil eye' whose jealousy had produced a curse.

We see the dangers of jealousy in the Bible too when King Saul's jealousy led him to attack David (1 Samuel 18:6–16). Yet, for all the evil and demonic activity which came from Saul's jealousy, the LORD was with David and protected him. As followers of 'great David's greater son', Jesus the Messiah, we also know of God's protection. Jesus has conquered evil through his death and resurrection. Therefore we don't need to fear people's envy or the evil eye, while we try to avoid being envious ourselves. We are able to share these truths with people like Ruhana and to pray that the Lord will call them and their families out of their fear-filled darkness.

Doing good deeds

> Live such good lives among the pagans that, though they accuse you of doing wrong, they may see your good deeds and glorify God on the day he visits us.
> (*Injil*, 1 Peter 2:12)

God's Word urges followers of Jesus the Messiah to do good to all people (Luke 6:27–36; 10:25–37; Galatians 6:10). Christians are told to bless others, not to insult or revile them, even when they do evil things to us (1 Peter 3:9). We must keep our 'tongue from evil' and our 'lips from deceitful speech' (1 Peter 3:10). We must 'seek peace' within a non-Christian world which may cause us great suffering (1 Peter 3:11; 4:7–19). All of this involves living out our religion every day of the week, not just on Sundays.

Through the centuries Christians have tried to do good to all people. For example, from early times, Christians looked after plague victims, despite the risk to themselves, because they knew that their home was in heaven. Indeed one pagan

Roman emperor, Julian (AD 360–363), complained that Christians supported not merely their own poor but the pagan poor as well.[1]

Moving from the time of Emperor Julian to that of Empress Victoria, we see people like George Müller energetically caring for the poor. The orphanages he established in Bristol, beginning in 1836, housed over 10,000 children. An 1871 article in *The Times* newspaper recorded that 23,000 children had been educated in his schools. In fact the education they received led to accusations that Müller was raising the poor above their rightful place in society!

Coming into the twenty-first century, Christians care for unborn children, the homeless, asylum seekers and the terminally ill. This isn't to say that Christian people get it right all the time and live infallibly perfect lives. Personally, I know I could have done much more good in my short life than I have done. However, as followers of Jesus we are to do good, because we have received God's mercy.

Submitting to authorities

> Submit yourselves for the Lord's sake to every authority instituted among men: whether to the king, as the supreme authority, or to governors, who are sent by him to punish those who do wrong and to commend those who do right.
> (*Injil*, 1 Peter 2:13–14)

The apostle Peter here was being practical. He realized that Christians were living in a world they didn't always rule. The believers he wrote to in Asia Minor (present-day Turkey) were a minority group in their country, as are many Christians today. The very next verses after he tells them to live 'good lives' (verse 12) concern this situation and give advice on how to live everyday life under other authorities, such as govern-ments (verses 13–17) and employers (verses 18–25).

Since God has established all earthly authorities (Daniel 2:21; 4:17; Romans 13:1–7), he is pleased when we submit to them. This includes submitting to governments and employers. It shows that we recognize God's ordained order for the world.

However, it isn't the case that God has one sphere of authority while the state has another! Some Muslim people suggest that Jesus teaches this in Mark 12:13–17. The context of this passage is crucial to understanding Jesus' words. A trap had been laid for Jesus in which his enemies hoped he would show himself to be either a traitor or a revolutionary. The first would mean that no-one would follow him, while the second could lead to his execution. So when the Jewish leaders asked him, 'Is it right to pay taxes to Caesar or not?' it wasn't a simple question about the role of the state and our responsibilities within it.

Jesus' response was astonishingly wise. He asked to see a coin, looked at the image on it and then said, 'Whose portrait is this?' This elicited the answer: 'Caesar's'. Jesus made a logical riposte: '[Therefore] Give to Caesar what is Caesar's and to God what is God's', which took him well clear of the horns of the dilemma. At one level, it was a brilliant piece of quick thinking which no-one could argue with – it's Caesar's coin so give it to him! However, it was more than this.

By talking about the image on the coin, Jesus was evoking God's words about humanity back at creation, when men and women were made in God's image. He was basically saying: 'If the coin has Caesar's image and belongs to him, then in whose image are you? And who do you belong to?' The answer is far-reaching: if we give back to God something that has his image on it, then we must equally give our whole selves to

God. Therefore we can see that there are not two separate and exclusive authorities – God and the state – because everything is under God, including ourselves.[2]

Submitting to earthly authorities also shows that we trust in God and therefore shows God to those around us. If we suffer under unjust authorities we are letting people see how God sustains us and keeps us going. This displays our belief that God and his heavenly kingdom are worth more than this life's pain. It declares God's praises and echoes the example of Jesus the Messiah who suffered unjustly in his life.

One example sprang to mind as I was thinking about this some more. A Christian friend who worked in a bank wrote a short booklet about applying investment principles to Jesus Christ to show that he was well worth following. He was able to publish this booklet and one morning left a copy on the desk of everyone who worked in his bank. Within a short time the human resources department (HR) contacted him saying that he had to remove all his booklets as they infringed the company's diversity policies. My friend had a choice to make: would he submit to his employer or not?

Recognizing that the employer was not commanding him to stop talking about Jesus and that taking back his booklet was not directly disobeying God, my friend submitted to his employer. He went to every desk to ask for the booklets back. Interestingly, when he said that HR didn't want people to have the booklet, many asked if they could keep it or fished it out of their bins because they were curious as to why HR wanted to censor their reading!

In this particular example, a Christian's submission to his employing authorities led to a good outcome. An attempt to prevent people from hearing about Jesus actually led to the opposite. As both the prophet Joseph and the first apostles realized, even though human beings may have bad intentions,

God can make things work out for good (Genesis 50:19–21; Acts 4:23–31).

Submission and honour in marriage

> Wives, in the same way be submissive to your husbands so that, if any of them do not believe the word, they may be won over without words by the behaviour of their wives, when they see the purity and reverence of your lives. Your beauty should not come from outward adornment, such as braided hair and the wearing of gold jewellery and fine clothes. Instead, it should be that of your inner self, the unfading beauty of a gentle and quiet spirit, which is of great worth in God's sight. For this is the way the holy women of the past who put their hope in God used to make themselves beautiful. They were submissive to their own husbands, like Sarah, who obeyed Abraham and called him her master. You are her daughters if you do what is right and do not give way to fear.
>
> Husbands, in the same way be considerate as you live with your wives, and treat them with honour as the weaker partner[3] and as heirs with you of the gracious gift of life, so that nothing will hinder your prayers.
> (*Injil*, 1 Peter 3:1–7)

Just as God has instituted government order, so he has established order between men and women. And just as we sometimes baulk at the idea of submitting to governments, so we sometimes shy away from submission within marriage. In our Western context we sometimes think that submission means denying equality, but the Bible keeps the two ideas in tension: it claims that someone can submit to authority and yet be equal in honour. Some genuine Christian people will disagree with me here, and you may be one of them, but I would encourage you to read on.[4] It is interesting to note that many Muslim people have less trouble with the pattern of marriage here than many twenty-first-century Western Christians.

John Piper explains a wife's submission like this: 'It is the disposition to follow a husband's authority and an inclination to yield to his leadership. It is an attitude that says, "I delight for you to take the initiative in our family. I am glad when you take responsibility for things and lead with love. I don't flourish when you are passive and I have to make sure the family works."'[5] As the apostle Paul makes clear in Ephesians 5:22–33, this kind of submission is modelled on the church's submission to Christ, just as the husband's loving leadership is based on Christ's sacrificial selflessness towards the church (and where such love is in evidence, it is much easier for a wife to submit).

The submission in 1 Peter is based on a wife's hope in God. This was how the Old Testament women of faith lived, such as Sarah, Abraham's wife. However, this does not at all mean that husbands are free to abuse their wives.

Husbands are to be considerate in the use of their authority towards their wives. They are to use their understanding to benefit their wives. They are to honour them. Their words, time, energy, money and very lives are for the wife's honour, not for themselves. While this isn't widely accepted within our culture, it is God's design for marriage and would tremendously benefit our communities.

Where are the details?

In response to hearing this, one friend, Hussein, argued that the Bible doesn't give enough details about how a husband is to live for God. Hussein told me that Islam lays down precise rules concerning how husbands should relate to their wives, even down to the importance of enabling her to breastfeed her children. This is a similar objection to the idea that Christianity is only for one day a week. What lies behind both is the feeling that Islam covers everyday life and Christianity does not.

I hope that I have shown so far that Christianity is not just for Sundays but for all days. Also the Bible does contain many detailed guidelines and pieces of wisdom on specific areas of life, such as how one treats property boundaries or brings up children.[6] To say that there are no details shows an ignorance of the Bible.

We should also recognize that neither Christianity nor Islam gives details for every area of life. I can't find anything in the Bible or Qur'an or Hadith (the sayings of Muhammad) which tells me how to use a personal computer. This doesn't mean that God is irrelevant because he has no comment to make on PCs. Instead, we realize that, like all technology, PCs can be used for good or bad and so we use them to serve others in as loving a way as possible. For example, we don't engage in internet porn or blogosphere gossip or online gambling. Rather we keep in touch with friends in far-off places, order gifts for people and spread the good news of Jesus more widely (as well as checking the football scores!).[7]

Finally, in some ways, details are unhelpful. Take husbands and wives, for example. A husband is to love his wife as Christ loved the church and gave himself up for her. This is the paradigm I am to work within in every area of my relationship with my wife. It should seep into every detail, from the time I get up in the morning, to conversation over breakfast, to caring for our children, to booking a holiday, to relating to my in-laws – all with the aim of putting my wife's needs above my own. These needs will differ from couple to couple and across cultures. Therefore God's Word gives us the over-arching and deeply challenging principle to live by. All the details of the married relationship need to be viewed from this perspective.

Reading God's Word and praying continually

To return to where we started this chapter, Christians do not pray and read the Bible only on a Sunday. The Scriptures urge us to read them so that we can grow in our knowledge and love of God. We are to be like newborn babies craving spiritual truth so that we can grow up in our faith (1 Peter 1:22 – 2:3). Babies wouldn't grow much on a Sunday-only feed and the same is true for followers of Jesus the Messiah.

God's Word also urges us to pray in all circumstances and to hand over our anxieties to God (1 Peter 5:7; Philippians 4:6; 1 Thessalonians 5:16–18). If we are in God's family and have been brought into his wonderful light, it is obvious that we should make the most of this access and continually be speaking to God in prayer. We do so to share our thoughts with him, to ask for his help, to confess our sins, to bring him our personal thanks and praise. We do so corporately on a Sunday, but also on our own in the quietness of an early morning in our bedroom or amid the noise of a busy commuter train. We do so 24/7 because we know that we are already God's people through his mercy and so he will listen to us. How we can be so certain is covered in the next chapter.

Key points

- Followers of Jesus the Messiah live every day for God's praise, not their own.
- They do so because God has already shown them mercy and not in order to receive his mercy.
- A life of praise should be seen daily, in our work, marriages, prayer and Bible reading.

Some questions

For followers of Jesus the Messiah

- Do you find yourself living for God on just one day of the week? If so, why is this?
- How does our identity in Jesus the Messiah help us to live 24/7 for him?
- Would your Muslim friend see you living for God 24/7?

For Muslim friends

- Why do you try to do good?
- In your heart of hearts, can you identify with the self-centredness of the crafty courtier in the tale?
- Why is knowing that you have received God's mercy a better incentive for doing good?

3. What sort of God can be murdered?

The certain victory of Jesus the Messiah

The death of God?

The nineteenth-century German philosopher Nietzsche claimed, 'God is dead. God remains dead. And we have killed him.'[1] Although he put these words into the mouth of a mad person, they were his own sentiments. More particularly, his writings claimed that Western science and rationalism had killed the Christian god. The Bible portrayed a god which didn't make sense to him (we will deal with this issue in the next chapter). For such a god to die, as Jesus did, made even less sense. This is the subject of the present chapter.

It may seem odd to begin with Nietzsche, but many Muslim people would share this philosopher's objections. A recent YouTube video which a Muslim friend sent to me reeled off staccato objections to the death of Jesus:

> What sort of god is one who can be murdered? Was god pleased with the murder or was he discontented? If he was discontented, was he not powerful enough to stop it? Who

answered people's prayers while god was dead? Were the heavens and skies vacated? Why didn't the angels help him? Was Christ revived by himself or another god? How can a grave enclose a god?

The death of Jesus forms one of the key objections which my Muslim friends have to the Christian message. It springs from Surah 4:157–158:

> [The Jews] said (in boast), 'We killed Christ Jesus the son of Mary, the Messenger of Allah' – but they killed him not, nor crucified him, but so it was made to appear to them, and those who differ therein are full of doubts, with no (certain) knowledge, but only conjecture to follow, for, of a surety they killed him not. No, Allah raised him up unto Himself; and Allah is Exalted in Power, Wise.

Foolishness and weakness versus wisdom and power

If the Christian faith is founded on Jesus' death and resurrection (and it is!), then this is an objection which must be taken seriously. If Christians live each day for God because they have already received God's mercy through Jesus' death and resurrection, then this life will make no sense to our Muslim friends until they have grasped the truth of Jesus' death and resurrection. Fortunately, Scripture is not unused to this objection. It is neither modern nor particularly Islamic:

> For the message of the cross is foolishness to those who are perishing, but to us who are being saved it is the power of God. For it is written [in Isaiah 29:14]:
>
>> I will destroy the wisdom of the wise;
>> the intelligence of the intelligent I will frustrate.

Where is the wise man? Where is the scholar? Where is the philosopher of this age? Has not God made foolish the wisdom of the world? For since in the wisdom of God the world through its wisdom did not know him, God was pleased through the foolishness of what was preached to save those who believe. Jews demand miraculous signs and Greeks look for wisdom, but we preach Christ crucified: a stumbling-block to Jews and foolishness to Gentiles, but to those whom God has called, both Jews and Greeks, Christ the power of God and the wisdom of God. For the foolishness of God is wiser than man's wisdom, and the weakness of God is stronger than man's strength.
(*Injil*, 1 Corinthians 1:18–25)

A crucified Messiah is a stumbling block for Jewish people when it comes to believing in Jesus. They cannot believe that Jesus is the Messiah because he was crucified.

In some ways, this is the opposite to Hussein's stumbling block at the crucifixion. He accepts that Jesus is the Messiah because the Qur'an gives him that title. However, this means that Jesus couldn't die because God would never let his Anointed One suffer like that.

The crucifixion appears foolish and weak to Hussein, if not downright blasphemous. At one particular meeting for better understanding, we spoke on the crucifixion (which one Muslim polemicist wittily called 'the cruci-fiction').[2] Hussein focused on how the Gospel evidence could not be trusted and that other so-called Gospels gave a true picture of Jesus.

Hussein's approach was similar to Dan Brown's in his novel *The Da Vinci Code* and has been effectively addressed elsewhere. Suffice to say, none of their evidence comes from the first century AD. Their 'Gospels' reflect a warping of the Christian message by people keen to introduce Greek philosophy and pagan ideas. They also disagree with the Scriptures revealed to previous prophets like Moses, David and Isaiah.[3] So, in order to truly understand why Jesus the Messiah was murdered, we must again start with the beginning of the Bible's story and come to the Gospels at the end.

Beginning with Moses

On Easter Sunday, a couple of Jesus' disciples were depressed at Jesus' death two days previously. They had thought that he would rescue Israel from Roman oppression. In a famous encounter with them on the road to Emmaus, the risen Jesus met them and said to them:

> 'How foolish you are, and how slow of heart to believe all that the prophets have spoken! Did not the Christ have to suffer these things and then enter his glory?' And beginning with Moses and all the Prophets, he explained to them what was said in all the Scriptures concerning himself.
>
> (*Injil*, Luke 24:25–27)

It must have been exciting for those two disciples to have their minds opened so that they understood the Scriptures correctly. Their hearts burned within them as they finally saw what was always there, from Genesis onwards. We don't know for sure what Jesus said to them, but if he began with Moses, he probably started in Genesis and helped them to have a proper understanding of sin and death.

Sin and death

Right at the beginning of the Bible, we are told that sin carries the penalty of death:

> The LORD God took the man and put him in the Garden of Eden to work it and take care of it. And the LORD God

commanded the man, 'You are free to eat from any tree in the
garden; but you must not eat from the tree of the knowledge
of good and evil, for when you eat of it you will surely die.'
(*Taurat*, Genesis 2:15–17)

Therefore, when Adam and Eve turned away from trusting
their loving Creator and preferred to believe a satanic lie, they
received God's just punishment of death. This death meant a
spiritual death (a broken relationship with their Creator and
exclusion from his beautiful paradise) as well as a physical
death. Sin carries the judicial penalty of death.

This penalty is seen in action as the prophet Moses records
divine history from Cain and Abel through Noah and down
to Abraham. Chapter 5 of Genesis, for example, lists the
descendants of Adam down to Noah, each concluding with
the refrain 'and then he died'. This drives home the point that
all people everywhere are now dying because there is sin in
the world. The widespread nature of sin leads God to say
that the inclinations of the thoughts of people's hearts are
only evil all of the time (Genesis 6:5). Therefore everyone
suffers death.

Mercy and fellowship

Alongside such justice, God also showed his mercy and compassion. God still wanted people to come near to him and live,
as Adam and Eve did in Genesis 2 when God walked with
them in Eden. His great mercy provided the way for this to
happen. God instituted sacrifices – based on the idea of an
animal dying in the place of a person – so that a person could
be cleaned of sin, God's punishment could be averted and
people could be brought close to God.

We begin to see this in the Cain and Abel story in Genesis
4 and more clearly as God provided a ram for Abraham's son

in Genesis 22. This story is picked up in the Qur'an (Surah 37:99–113) and is celebrated during the time of pilgrimage as *Qurbani Eid*, the festival which is about 'bringing together' or 'fellowship with God'.[4]

In Genesis 22 God asks Abraham to kill his only son whom he loves. Most Muslim people think that the son in the story was Ishmael.[5] However, the Qur'an doesn't say explicitly that the intended sacrifice was Ishmael. It only says 'son' without ever naming him. The Bible is very clear that Ishmael and his mother Hagar were not with Abraham at this stage. Also, while God did bless Ishmael (Genesis 17:20), Isaac was considered to be the son or heir of God's everlasting promises and blessings to Abraham (Genesis 17:19, 21). Therefore it was Isaac who was considered to be Abraham's one and only, unique son. Abraham showed his devotion to God by being prepared to offer this unique son to God, which was all the more remarkable considering the future blessings he was intended to bring.

In the awful scene depicted in Genesis 22:9–10, Abraham placed his beloved son on an altar, tied him down, raised the knife – and was just about to plunge it down when God called out for him to stop. God now knew that Abraham feared him and God in turn provided the right sacrifice.

Abraham lifted his eyes from the altar and saw a ram caught in a bush by its horns. He took the ram and offered it instead of his son. This is the key point: the ram provided by God was offered instead of the child (Genesis 22:13).

God provided a way for Abraham's son not to be killed. The ram 'ransomed' or 'redeemed' or 'delivered' or 'replaced' his son (all different ways of translating the Arabic word *kaffara* according to Yusuf Ali's footnote on Surah 37:107).[6] God's mercy and compassion were seen in his provision of a ransoming sacrifice which achieved *qurbani*. It allowed Abraham to come near to God. This set the ongoing pattern for God's people, enabling them to relate to their Creator.

Therefore we see God's people ransomed from Egypt and God's judgment through the sacrificial death of a lamb. As God saw that a death had taken place in a particular household, he passed over that family's sin and punished their Egyptian enemies with death instead. This Passover ransomed the people of Israel from slavery, another *kaffara* (Exodus 11:1 – 12:51). It brought them close to God (Exodus 19:3–6), another *qurbani*.

God's people still sinned and therefore God instituted daily and yearly animal sacrifices (Leviticus 4:1 – 6:7; 16:1 – 17:9). Through these frequent sacrifices the people's sins were not punished as they deserved, but an animal died instead. Consequently, the holy God was able to live with his people. He was *at one* with his people. This is where we get the word 'atonement', which is similar to the idea of 'bringing near' or *qurbani*.

It's not an exaggeration to say that there was a lot of blood and death around God's people in the time of the prophet Moses, but it was necessary. If people are not to experience God's death sentence spiritually, physically and eternally themselves, then a sacrifice needs to take place. Later Bible prophets deepened this concept further as we see below.

Moving to the Prophets

As God progressively revealed his plans through his prophets, God's people were told that a better sacrifice was coming. This sacrifice wouldn't need to be repeated day after day and year after year. This sacrifice would finally do away with sin and completely take away God's punishment for our rebellion against him.

Cleaned from sin

The prophet Zechariah, writing around 520 BC, gives us various prophecies about this. One day God will completely clean people from sin (Zechariah 3:8–10). God gives a promise sealed in blood which will set people free (9:11). God's mercy will be received through 'one they have pierced' (12:10). God's Shepherd will be struck down (13:7).

The prophet Isaiah, writing around 700 BC, has a crucial prophecy too. The Servant of God will be despised, rejected, wounded, killed and put in a grave (Isaiah 53:3, 8, 9). The Servant will die for his people's sins (53:5, 6, 12). His wounds will bring a healed relationship with God (53:5).

It is often argued (using Bible references like Ezekiel 18) that it is unjust for one person to die for the sins of another and that individuals bear the responsibility for their own sins.[7] However, sometimes this can just be an excuse not to look at the evidence, so I would encourage people first to evaluate the evidence given here and then read Ezekiel in its context.

Intriguingly, it was God's will to crush the Servant (Isaiah 53:9–10) and yet God's plan did not end in death (53:10–11). In a couple of recent meetings for better understanding on this topic, the Muslim speaker argued that 'the Servant' means Israel. While the identity of the Servant in Isaiah is in some ways veiled – he is both Israel and Jesus at various levels – it cannot mean 'Israel' in Isaiah 53.

First, the pronouns deny this. Throughout chapter 53 *he* does something for *us*; for example,

> . . . the LORD has laid on *him*
> the iniquity of *us* all . . .

> for the transgression of *my* people *he* was stricken.
> (verses 6, 8, my italics)

Second, the Servant

> had done no violence,
>> nor was any deceit in his mouth.
> (verse 9)

Yet throughout Isaiah and the whole Old Testament we read of Israel's deceit, violence and sinfulness. The Servant prophesied here is clearly one person and not Israel.

An end to sin

The two prophets Zechariah and Isaiah were looking forward to an eternally effective sacrifice. In between them was the prophet Daniel. He lived as an exile in Babylon in the sixth century BC. One day while he was praying and confessing his sins, the angel Gabriel appeared to him and said:

> Seventy 'sevens' are decreed for your people and your holy city *to finish transgression, to put an end to sin, to atone for wickedness, to bring in everlasting righteousness*, to seal up vision and prophecy and to anoint the most holy place.
>
> Know and understand this: From the issuing of the decree to restore and rebuild Jerusalem until the Anointed One, the ruler, comes, there will be seven 'sevens', and sixty-two 'sevens'. It will be rebuilt with streets and a trench, but in times of trouble. After the sixty-two 'sevens', *the Anointed One will be cut off [but not for himself]*. The people of the ruler who will come will destroy the city and the sanctuary. The end will come like a flood: War will continue until the end, and desolations have been decreed. *He will confirm a covenant with many* for one 'seven'. In the middle of the 'seven' *he will put an end to sacrifice and offering*.
> (Prophet Daniel 9:24–27, my italics; words in square brackets are an alternative reading of the text)

This is a tricky passage, but the important points are high-lighted in italics. The angel Gabriel is saying in effect: 'A time is coming when the sins you have been worrying about and which stare God in the face will be gone. The sins which cry out for punishment and which separate people from the holy God will be removed from his sight and atoned for.' How will this happen?

It comes about when the Anointed One (which is what 'Messiah' means in Hebrew or 'Christ' in Greek) is 'cut off but not for himself'. The prophet Isaiah talks about someone being cut off for sins but not for his own (Isaiah 53:8, 12), and this is what the angel Gabriel seems to be getting at here as well – especially because it will put an end to all other sacrifices.

Therefore, from God, via the angel Gabriel, through the prophet Daniel, we are being told that an Anointed One will be the sacrifice to bring an end to sin. This sacrifice will bring many people near to God in everlasting righteousness.

Finishing with the Psalms

This idea that an Anointed One would suffer as the leader of God's people is also seen throughout the Psalms of David (written from around 1000 BC). Psalms often depict God's anointed ruler suffering at the hands of his enemies. In Psalm 22 King David describes a future event when a kingly person will suffer:[8]

All who see me mock me;
    they hurl insults, shaking their heads:
'He trusts in the LORD;
    let the LORD rescue him;
Let him deliver him,
    since he delights in him' . . .

Dogs have surrounded me;
  a band of evil men has encircled me,
  they have pierced my hands and my feet.
I can count all my bones;
  people stare and gloat over me.
They divide my garments among them
  and cast lots for my clothing.
  (*Zabur*, Psalm 22:7–8, 16–18)

The Psalms of David also include descriptions of the Messiah being vindicated. His body is not allowed to 'see decay' (Psalm 16:10). This means that it will not decompose in the grave. Also, the Messiah will rule over all nations forever and will destroy those who oppose him (Psalms 2:4–12; 110).

Therefore, beginning with Moses and continuing through the Prophets and the Psalms, we can see that God promised to provide a perfect sacrifice of his Anointed One which would last for all eternity, taking away sin and bringing people near to God. Now we can at last turn to Jesus' crucifixion to see these promises coming to fruition.

The crucified Christ opens up paradise

At the beginning of Matthew's Gospel, the angel Gabriel appears again. He tells Joseph that his wife will have a son who will save his people from their sins (Matthew 1:21). The crucifixion of Jesus Christ, the Anointed One, fulfilled these words of Gabriel to Joseph and his earlier words to the prophet Daniel. Here is Luke's account of the crucifixion as his narrative draws together the blood-red threads from Moses, the Prophets and the Psalms:

Two other men, both criminals, were also led out with him to be executed. When they came to the place called the Skull, there they crucified him, along with the criminals – one on his right, the other on his left. Jesus said, 'Father, forgive them, for they do not know what they are doing.' And they divided up his clothes by casting lots.

The people stood watching, and the rulers even sneered at him. They said, 'He saved others; let him save himself if he is the Christ of God, the Chosen One.'

The soldiers also came up and mocked him. They offered him wine vinegar and said, 'If you are the king of the Jews, save yourself.'

There was a written notice above him, which read: THIS IS THE KING OF THE JEWS.

One of the criminals who hung there hurled insults at him: 'Aren't you the Christ? Save yourself and us!'

But the other criminal rebuked him. 'Don't you fear God,' he said, 'since you are under the same sentence? We are punished justly, for we are getting what our deeds deserve. But this man has done nothing wrong.'

Then he said, 'Jesus, remember me when you come into your kingdom.'

Jesus answered him, 'I tell you the truth, today you will be with me in paradise.'

It was now about the sixth hour, and darkness came over the whole land until the ninth hour, for the sun stopped shining. And the curtain of the temple was torn in two. Jesus called out with a loud voice, 'Father, into your hands I commit my spirit.' When he had said this, he breathed his last.

(*Injil*, Luke 23:32–46)

As Psalm 22 predicted, God's Anointed One was mocked and his clothes were divided among his enemies. Like the Suffering Servant of Isaiah 53 and Daniel 9, the innocent Jesus was cut off for sins, but not for his own. And in an amazing way, Jesus' death brought access to God and his paradise.

Jesus' death caused the curtain in the temple to be torn in two. The curtain was a real physical barrier that was also hugely symbolic. Behind it was the place where the holy God lived, and only one man, the high priest, could go behind it. He could do so only once a year, on the Day of Atonement, and only when sacrifices for sin had taken place (Leviticus 16). When that curtain was ripped apart, it was a striking demonstration that people could now enter God's presence and that the temple's sacrifices had ended.

One thief recognized who Jesus really was. Through Jesus' death this repentant thief could now enter paradise and come near to God. The death that God demanded for sin had taken place. The eternal 'bringing together' with God, or *qurbani*, had occurred so that this thief, and anyone else who turns to this crucified Messiah, could receive God's forgiveness and everlasting righteousness.

Even more amazingly, we know that the good news did not end there. The tomb in which Jesus was laid was soon empty. He was raised from the dead and vindicated as God's Anointed One and Ruler over the nations, just as Moses, the Prophets and the Psalms said would happen.

Through Jesus' death and resurrection our great enemy's sting has been neutered. Punishment and the second death in hell are no more. Satan's accusations against us have no power because our guilt and shame have been taken away. Jesus has disarmed the evil powers and authorities through his triumph at the cross. This means that we can be sure of the mercy and protection we looked at in the last chapter. Therefore we can live for God without fear of evil or of failure.

A holistic answer

A biblical theme
Using the whole Bible in this way helps us to see that Jesus' death and resurrection was not something fabricated by the Gospel writers, but is at the centre of God's Word. It is the thread which holds it all together. It would be impossible to fabricate the different prophetic writings which we have outlined above, written over so many different eras. To say that the crucifixion is made up is to ignore all this evidence. Also, the Gospels themselves are authentic eyewitness testimony. We can trust them.

Qur'anic problems
The usual Islamic interpretation of Surah 4:157 is that Jesus appeared to be on the cross, but it was actually someone made to look like him. Chawcat Moucarry highlights some difficulties with this in his book *Faith to Faith* as he looks at what the famous Muslim philosopher and theologian al-Razi thought about this issue.[9]

Razi (1149–1209) recognized that denying Jesus' crucifixion when people saw Jesus crucified means that we live in a world where we cannot be sure of anything. Furthermore, as Razi affirmed, the Gospel accounts of the crucifixion rely on eyewitness testimony in much the same way as the Qur'an and the records of Muhammad's own life. How can we be sure of the eyewitness testimony about these things?

Razi also wondered why, if Jesus was as powerful as both the Qur'an and the Gospels testify, he didn't prevent his capture rather than be captured and then substituted. Surely it would have been easier to evade capture as he had done before. God could have taken Jesus from the earth without having to put someone else on the cross on his place. Why did an innocent third party have to die? Indeed why did that person not tell everyone that he was not Jesus?

After listing these difficulties, Razi was unable to provide any conclusive answers. Instead, he resigned himself to assert that the Qur'an cannot be contradicted. However, there is a potential problem here too.

Other verses in the Qur'an seem to indicate that Jesus would die; for example, Surah 19:33:

> [Jesus said]: 'So peace is on me the day I was born, the day that I die and the day that I shall be raised up to life (again).'

This verse compares with Surah 19:15:

> [Speaking about John the Baptist]: So Peace on him the day he was born, the day he dies, and the day that he will be raised to life (again).

These verses suggest that Jesus' route of birth, death and resurrection is similar to John the Baptist's. It is not a case of Jesus being born, being raised to heaven, then returning to earth, then dying and then being raised again. Both verses have a chronology in view and Jesus' life/death/raised chronology follows John the Baptist's. Therefore, just as John the Baptist was born, suffered a martyr's death and then will be raised to life, so too for Jesus the Messiah. The big difference is that John the Baptist still awaits his physical resurrection, while Jesus' tomb is empty and his work has been vindicated.

Prophets do suffer

The example of John the Baptist also helps us to see that it is not unusual for God's prophets to suffer death and humiliation at the hands of their enemies. Some Muslim people think that

God would never allow his prophets to suffer in such ways, but history shows us that God's prophets did suffer. John the Baptist languished in prison and then had his head put on a platter by King Herod. Jesus himself made the point that God's spokesmen had always been persecuted, from Abel onwards (Matthew 23:34–35; Luke 11:49–51). Indeed, this pattern of suffering *now* with resurrection and glorious vindication *to come* is one which followers of Jesus have to take too (Matthew 16:24–27; Hebrews 11).

As I spoke with Hussein about these kinds of things, he realized that his case against the crucifixion would need to be much stronger. He now had to engage with the whole Bible, not just the Gospels; an empty tomb, not just a cross; the veracity of any eyewitnesses, not just those at the cross; and the Qur'an's own testimony that Jesus would be born, die and rise again.

Forgiving enemies

Hussein remains unconvinced, but one friend, Ishaq, recognized his need for salvation from his sins. As a student in Pakistan he was reading a book of quotations, when one sentence made him suddenly stop: '"Love your enemies" (Jesus Christ).' These words seared into his heart and lodged there for many years. How could anyone say such things? *To love one's enemies is impossible! It's certainly not true in my religion*, he thought.

Over time Ishaq moved to the UK and became more aware of his unworthiness before God. He could find no way of atoning for his sins, despite being devout in his daily, weekly and yearly religious observances. 'Love your enemies' burned away some more, until he came to see that the person who said these words had also practised them. He even did so for the sake of sinners like him.

Ishaq realized that, at the cross, Jesus Christ was prepared to forgive his most bitter enemies. He recognized that, at the cross, Jesus the Messiah showed astounding love for people who rejected his kingship. He came to trust that Jesus' death and resurrection was the eternal *kaffara* he needed and that he could have certain fellowship with the Creator and covenant-keeping God of the universe. Such certainty has enabled him to live each day doing good to all, even to those who have opposed him for his new faith.

Key points

- All of Scripture shows us that sin deserves death and that God promised a sacrifice so that his people would not have to suffer that death.
- God provided the necessary sacrifice in Jesus the Messiah's death and resurrection.
- This work of God certainly brings us into God's family.

Some questions

For followers of Jesus the Messiah

- In order to understand Jesus' death and resurrection, we must understand the seriousness of sin. How does Genesis 1 – 3 help us to see sin's seriousness?
- If you were to read Genesis 3 with a Muslim friend, what would you want to highlight?
- How could you show the necessity of a sacrifice for people from the story of Abraham and his son in Genesis 22?

For Muslim friends

- If God punishes sin through death, what does this show us about sin? What effects did sin have for Adam and Eve?
- Why did God institute sacrifices?
- If you do not think that Jesus the Messiah died and rose again, which pieces of evidence do you distrust? Why?

4. What sort of God can be born as a baby?

The Word took on human form

Who is your God?

Some years ago, two friends and I set up a Christian booktable in East London during Ramadan. Some people did not like the idea of us doing this, but through it a number of good friendships with Muslim men developed. The first night we were there, I can remember one older, tramp-like man coming up to the table. The area was known for its homeless and alcohol problems. Wrongly judging by appearances, I expected some slurred speech and abuse, but instead was told 'God does not beget, nor is he begotten.' The man then explained that this meant that God could not be a father nor have a son. This in turn led to some ridicule of the Christian idea that God could come to earth, eat, drink, sleep and go to the toilet.

The words this man spoke sprang from Surah 112:3, which was one of the first surahs which Muhammad preached. The title of the Surah is *Al-Ikhlas* or 'The Purity of Faith'. It consists of just four short verses and emphasizes that Allah is God alone and that there is nothing in creation like him. It appears to have come to Muhammad while he was in Mecca and was calling pagans from polytheism to follow one God. Yusuf Ali's footnote says that the begetting verse is meant 'to negate the Christian idea of the godhead',[1] much as the man at the booktable said. It appears inscribed in many mosques, including the Dome of the Rock in Jerusalem.

Whether or not this was originally intended as a polemic against Christians, we do need to help our Muslim friends to understand what we mean when we say things like 'God came to earth', 'God died on the cross' and 'Jesus is the Son of God'. We need to help our friends see how the God who is Creator, Ruler and personal Covenant-Maker (chapter 1) is also the God who promised and planned that Jesus should die for sins (chapter 3). One of the ways we can do this is by bringing those two themes together in Jesus who is the fully divine, fully human, eternal Word of the Most High.

The almighty God who lived with his people in the Old Testament

Orthodox Muslim people usually think that it is impossible for humanity to live with God. He is so supreme and so separate or 'other' from his creation,

> And there is none like unto him.
> (Surah 112:4)

Imams that I have spoken to suggest that even in the Islamic paradise, where its people are forgiven in some way, God is not present because the Creator is far beyond his creation. As we saw in chapter 1, touching on the idea of analogies, this is not how the holy Bible describes God to us. The Scriptures describe a God who is unlike his creation (transcendent, such as in Isaiah 40:18) and also able to be with his creation (immanent, such as in Isaiah 40:1–5).

The Bible introduces us to the God who is uncreated, yet he made humanity in his image (Genesis 1:26–27). Therefore we are like him in some way and God is not completely 'other'.

God walked with Adam

In Genesis 2 we see that God is the Ruler over his creation, yet he is also personally involved with the people he has made as he *talks* to Adam. In Genesis 3 God omnipotently judged Adam and Eve's disobedience, yet was used to *walking with them* in Eden. That point is very significant. It shows that God's paradise was glorious not just because of its abundant blessings to Adam and Eve, but also because God lived there with his people. The transcendent Creator enjoyed walking with his creatures.

In Genesis 11, as Adam's descendants gathered together at Babel to make a name for themselves and challenge God, God *came down to see* their city, tower and rebellion, and punished them by scattering them across the globe. His transcendent power was worked out through his immanent sight of the people.

God appeared to Abraham

After God had revealed to Abraham his rescue plan of blessing the nations (Genesis 12 –15) and promised that Isaac would be the heir of these promises (Genesis 17), we are told that

> The LORD appeared to Abraham near the great trees of Mamre while he was sitting at the entrance to his tent in the heat of the day. Abraham looked up and saw three men standing nearby. When he saw them, he hurried from the entrance of his tent to meet them and bowed low to the ground.
>
> (*Taurat*, Genesis 18:1–2)

Abraham hosted these three people in his tent and they *ate* with him. Two of the three were angels, but the third is said to have been God himself (18:10, 33; 19:1). This God also *knew* what Sarah was thinking and doing while she stood outside the tent (18:10–15). This is another example of God as a person showing divine knowledge as well as earthly presence. We see this too as the LORD *appeared* to the other patriarchs, Isaac and Jacob (26:24; 32:30).

God came near to Moses

This pattern is repeated with the prophet Moses as God *appeared* to him in a burning bush and said that *he had come down* to rescue his people from Egypt (Exodus 3:1–15). He physically *came near* to Moses and also showed both knowledge of the future and control over the present, not least through defeating Pharaoh. Later on, as the people of Israel rebelled against their rescuing God, God threatened *not to go with them* because they were so stubborn and rebellious (33:1–6). However, the LORD *revealed* himself (again!) to Moses, showing that he was full of steadfast love and faithfulness, and *did go with* Israel.

Exodus concludes with God's glory *settling upon* and *filling* a special tent or tabernacle which God had commanded the Israelites to build (Exodus 40). Later on, the temple in Jerusalem replaced the tabernacle and God's glory *descended* there too, as King Solomon testified (1 Kings 8:10–11).

God lives in heaven and on earth

The book of the prophet Isaiah is full of descriptions of God's glorious transcendence and sovereign power. In many ways, Isaiah's writings could be described as the high point of Old Testament monotheism. For example:

Remember the former things, those of long ago;
    I am God, and there is no other;
    I am God, and there is none like me.
I make known the end from the beginning,
    from ancient times, what is still to come.
I say: My purpose will stand,
    and I will do all that I please.
(Prophet Isaiah 46:9–10)

And yet such high points are alongside descriptions of God personally *comforting* his people and *coming to them* (Isaiah 40:1–5). Indeed this God lives both in heaven and on earth:

For this is what the high and lofty One says –
    he who lives for ever, whose name is holy:
'I live in a high and holy place,
    but also with him who is contrite and lowly in spirit,
to revive the spirit of the lowly
    and to revive the heart of the contrite.'
(Prophet Isaiah 57:15)

All this is to show that the idea of God coming to earth to be with his people is rooted in the Old Testament Scriptures. This is not an idea Christians made up after Jesus the Messiah had walked the earth or at the Council of Nicea or any other time. The examples of God living with his people are all part of the Hebrew Scriptures which pre-date both Christianity and Islam. These would be agreed upon by Jewish people who are not following a crucified Messiah. Again, we must remember that the life of Jesus Christ didn't come out of nowhere. It was part of an ongoing revelation of God and was in keeping with this.

The almighty God who lived with his people in the New Testament

'The Word became flesh'

In view of these hundreds of years of God's revelation prior to Jesus Christ walking the earth, it is no surprise that one of Jesus' closest friends, the apostle John, wrote (under God's inspiration):

> The Word became flesh and made his dwelling among us. We have seen his glory, the glory of the One and Only, who came from the Father, full of grace and truth.
>
> John [the Baptist] testifies concerning him. He cries out, saying, 'This was he of whom I said, "He who comes after me has surpassed me because he was before me."' From the fulness of his grace we have all received one blessing after another. For the law was given through Moses; grace and truth came through Jesus Christ. No-one has ever seen God, but God the One and Only, who is at the Father's side, has made him known. (*Injil*, John 1:14–18)

These words are deliberate echoes of Moses and the rescue from Egypt. 'Made his dwelling' is literally 'tabernacled'. 'Glory' picks up the revelation of God's glory at Mount Sinai to Moses. 'Grace' and 'truth' are Greek translations of 'steadfast love' and 'faithfulness' which the LORD told Moses were defining features of his character. At Mount Sinai God revealed his goodness, describing himself as

> The LORD, the LORD, the compassionate and gracious God, slow to anger, abounding in *love and faithfulness*, maintaining love to thousands, and forgiving wickedness, rebellion and sin. (*Taurat*, Exodus 34:6–7, my italics)

The highlighted pair of expressions recurs again and again in the Old Testament. The two words that John uses, describing Jesus as full of 'grace and truth', are his ways of summing up the same ideas.[2]

John mentions Moses' law to compare it to the truth brought by Jesus – not putting them in opposition to each other, but making an argument from something less important to something much greater. He is basically saying: 'If Moses brought blessing, then how much greater is the blessing which Jesus has brought!' Finally, John explains that Moses didn't truly see God on Mount Sinai, but Jesus has seen God and so can fully reveal him to the world.

The apostle John wrote these words having been prepared by the Old Testament and after reflecting on the Jesus he had known, loved and lived with for more than three years. He had seen Jesus' power over creation: turning water into wine, feeding over 5,000 people, walking on water and attracting fish into his followers' nets (John 2:1–11; 6:5–13, 19–21; 21:1–11 respectively). He had seen Jesus heal an official's son who was close to death, a man paralysed for thirty-eight years and a man born blind (John 4:46–54; 5:1–9; 9:1–7 respectively). He was there when Jesus raised his friend Lazarus to life (John 11:1–44). The apostle John saw Jesus doing God-like things and so concluded that this was God who had come to be with his people. He realized that the powerful Word of God which had created life back in Genesis 1 was the person in front of him, who showed control over all of life.

Divine power and claims
Some Muslim people say that this doesn't show Jesus' divinity because Moses and Elisha did similar things by God's power. For example, the Qur'an states that Jesus did these things by Allah's permission rather than by himself (Surah 5:110). While

it is true that Moses and Elisha did similar miracles to Jesus, many of Jesus' miracles were done in a way unlike these other prophets. Many of Jesus' miracles involved no calling on God or prayer, but Jesus simply did what he wanted to.

In John's Gospel, for example, when Jesus brought his dead friend Lazarus back to life he didn't ask God's permission to do so. Jesus did speak to God first, but he prayed so that the crowd would see that he was truly sent from the Father in heaven and wasn't a rival to him (we will look at this issue further in chapter 5 of this book). Jesus simply gave a command and it happened the way he said, just as God did back in Genesis 1 when he created the universe.

Also, Moses and Elisha continually pointed people to the God they should be following, while Jesus pointed to himself as more than human and said that people should believe in him as the way to receive life (see John 3, for example). It is also noticeable in John's Gospel that Jesus' words often deliberately pick up the name of God revealed in the Old Testament and claim it for himself. An example of this is found in John 10 where Jesus calls himself 'the good shepherd', much like a description of the LORD God in Isaiah 40:11. He is also the 'great I AM' nine times in John's Gospel, which picks up the nine times that name for God occurs in the Old Testament.[3]

Jesus cannot be seen simply as a prophet because he is much more than this. He is not at odds with the God who gave and sustained the lives of his people in the Old Testament yet also visited them in tents and burning bushes. He is one who has high and lofty power and yet came to be with the humble and lowly.

The God who took on a physical body
If Jesus Christ was a continuation of the process in which God revealed himself, it is no surprise that an angel announced his

birth or that choirs of angels sang as he entered the world. Jesus' miraculous virgin birth in itself didn't make him divine. Nor is it the case that God had sex with Mary to produce a divine son (even though at times the Qur'an seems to suggest that Christians think this).[4] However, if Jesus is divine then it isn't surprising that he took on a physical body in this way.

This again helps us to see that Jesus Christ must be more than a prophet, but why did God come to earth in this way? After all, God had stepped into creation before without needing to become fully human. For an answer to this, we again need to go back to the beginning.

The 'divine dilemma'[5]

The LORD God created Adam and Eve to live in his world and to rule over it. King David recognized this fact and praised God for it:

> You made him [humankind] ruler over the works
>   of your hands;
>   you put everything under his feet:
> all flocks and herds,
>   and the beasts of the field,
> the birds of the air,
>   and the fish of the sea,
>   all that swim the paths of the seas.
> (Zabur, Psalm 8:6–8)

God commanded Adam and Eve to have many offspring and to cultivate the world (Genesis 1:28–30). They and all of humanity were intended to rule over God's good world and under his good command as his vicegerents.[6] That is, they would rule the earth with a delegated authority – they would still be under God, who had a higher authority. To show that

God was still in overall charge he set good limits on his vice-gerents by commanding them not to eat from the tree of the knowledge of good and evil or else they would die (Genesis 2:16–17).

Now we have a problem. As we know, Adam and Eve did eat from the tree and so deserved death. However, God had said that they and their descendants would be rulers over the earth.

How could God be true to both of these competing promises? How could men and women live as rulers *and* die as rebels? How could they be *both* corrupted mortal beings *and* also rule forever as God intended? Could God go back on his word so that humans would die and not rule? Or could God go back on his word so that humans would rule and not die? This has been described as the 'divine dilemma'.

Repentance is not enough

Some Muslim people would say that all Adam and Eve had to do was to repent and that would turn them from rebels into rightful rulers. However, this is not a solution, for at least three reasons.

First, while orthodox Islam does teach that Adam and Eve repented, they were not returned to paradise. Repentance didn't fully work. It didn't bring about complete restoration to their state of paradise. They didn't have a perfect relation-ship with God or their world. Their sin led to a change in their circumstances which repentance did not fully solve. Adam and Eve had to live and die as part of the world under God's judgment.

Second, repentance would not remove God from his binding word. He would be untrue to himself if people did not die. He had said that disobedience against him would lead to death.

Third, once sin entered the world, it spread and did not remain as one act of rebellion. As we have seen in previous chapters, sin spread like cancer, leading to an ongoing downward spiral of death and corruption. Therefore, repentance could not meet the demands laid upon it by sin, death and corruption. Something greater was needed.

The divine solution

This 'something greater' was a Someone far greater – the Word of God (a title which the Qur'an gives to Jesus in Surah 3:45). Rather than entering our world in an angelic form, as appears to be the case in some appearances in the Old Testament described above, the Word took on a physical body through the virgin Mary and God's Holy Spirit. Out of love for humanity, the Word became a real human being with a body which 'was liable to the corruption of death',[7] as the early church leader Athanasius put it, so that death might be taken away.

> The Word perceived that corruption could not be got rid of otherwise than through death; yet He Himself, as the Word, being immortal and the Father's Son, was such as could not die. For this reason, therefore, He assumed a body capable of death, in order that it, through belonging to the Word Who is above all, might become in dying a sufficient exchange for all.[8]

In addition, when the Word took on a physical body, he also showed what a true human being should look like. Jesus Christ, the Word who 'became flesh', lived a perfect life and so was justly able to be the right ruler of the world, as Adam should have been. The Qur'an recognizes that Jesus is similar to Adam (Surah 3:59) because Adam too came from the word of God rather than through a human father, but Jesus is also much greater than Adam.

In contrast to Adam, who was intended to rule over creation but failed, Jesus is the right ruler through his sinless obedience to God. (His holiness is recognized in Surah 19:19.) One of the reasons why Jesus was tempted by Satan was to show that he was greater than Adam and would not succumb to temptation (Luke 3:23 – 4:13). Indeed, as we have seen in earlier chapters, Jesus came in order to defeat our enemy the devil. Having done so, he is able to help us in our temptations too:

> Since the children have flesh and blood, he [Jesus] too shared in
> their humanity so that by his death he might destroy him who
> holds the power of death – that is, the devil – and free those
> who all their lives were held in slavery by their fear of death.
> For surely it is not angels he helps, but Abraham's descendants.
> For this reason he had to be made like his brothers in every
> way, in order that he might become a merciful and faithful high
> priest in service to God, and that he might make atonement for
> the sins of the people. Because he himself suffered when he
> was tempted, he is able to help those who are being tempted.
> (*Injil*, Hebrews 2:14–18)

Adam shows the need for a greater man, one like him but pure. Although Adam was fully human, he didn't fulfil his God-given role. In some ways, Adam was like a shadow human pointing towards the most fully human Jesus. Jesus' complete obedience showed that he is much greater than Adam's pale shadow. Jesus is the faithful high priest who serves God in ways Adam did not. As another early church leader put it, Jesus is the 'recapitulation' of Adam.[9] It is as if Adam was the draft outline in pencil which was finally inked in by the perfect version, Jesus.

The divine presence

Within folk Islam there is a feeling that God is so 'other' and transcendent that he cannot possibly be interested in the day-to-day realities of ordinary people. This is even the case within orthodox Islam. God is said to be as close to you as your jugular vein, but this is only so that he can record your thoughts for Judgment Day (Surah 50:16–17). The wonderful thing about the Christian Scriptures is that they show God to be really this close. He is very much involved in his people's lives, providing a deeper picture of his character than the Qur'an appears to know, although it seems to hint at it. He visited his people frequently in the Old Testament. He even lived on earth with his people as the Second Adam (Jesus). He knows what it's like to live in this world.

He has suffered. He has been lonely. He has been shamed. He has felt others' revenge. Therefore, he is able to understand men and women and sympathize with them.

He is able to understand our pain and our temptations. We don't need to turn to other mediators or forms of security or ministers or imams or amulets or special incantations because we have a God who knows and cares. Jesus is our great mediator. He fulfils the role of one of the Old Testament's key mediators between people and God, the high priest, by acting on behalf of his people:

> For we do not have a high priest who is unable to sympathise with our weaknesses, but we have one who has been tempted in every way, just as we are – yet was without sin. Let us then approach the throne of grace with confidence, so that we may receive mercy and find grace to help us in our time of need.
>
> (*Injil*, Hebrews 4:15–16)

God crucified

Many Muslim people struggle to understand how Christian people can claim that Jesus is divine and yet walked the earth. Their presupposition appears to be that 'divinity is attribute *x* and Jesus does not fit into this *x*'. However, that is not how the Bible operates.

Through his prophets, God has revealed himself as the one who walked with his people in Eden, warned Cain personally, met with Abraham, wrestled with Jacob and revealed himself to Moses. This God involved himself with the dust and dirt of this world. Can Jesus fit into this identity? Yes, and resoundingly so.

The councils of Nicea and Chalcedon in the fourth and fifth centuries AD were helpful in drawing out explanations and distinctions about Jesus' identity. That said, we don't need them in order to be convinced that the God of the Old Testament is consistent with Jesus Christ of the New Testament and leads us to him. Because God is personal and lives with his people, so the Word of God took on a physical body. Therefore Jesus' birth was announced by angels, his character was pure, his actions were powerful, his death was staggering and his resurrection was wonderful.

Can God die in such a staggering way? No, not if you think that death means an end to existence. However, death doesn't mean that in the Bible, as we saw in the last chapter.

In the Bible, death is a temporary end to someone's physical body and it is also a disruption in a person's relationship with God. Adam and Eve suffered the death of their relationship with God on the day that they disobeyed him, and they experienced the death of their bodies when they took their last breath. Neither of these deaths meant that they ceased to exist, as even now their souls are waiting for the day of resurrection and final judgment. Could Jesus as God's Son experience both types of death? Yes, as he took his last physical breath and as he faced being abandoned spiritually by his Father for the sin with which he was identifying.

God revealed

Jesus' death on the cross is also the place where we see most clearly who God is. At the cross we see God truly identifying with his creatures, showing love and mercy, defeating Satan and death, living with lowly people, fulfilling his covenant promises and completing his plan of salvation. Jesus himself makes that explicit in John's Gospel.

> So Jesus said to them, 'When you have lifted up the Son of Man, then you will know that I am he . . . '
> (*Injil*, John 8:28 ESV)

The first people to believe in this message were Jewish people. Jewish monotheists of the first century were able to accept the idea that Jesus was the Word of God in a human body because they understood who the God of the Old Testament was. It wasn't a case of God *taking a son* to him-self,[10] but rather that the eternal Word or Son took *'flesh'* to himself. So Peter and the other apostles could preach from the very beginning:

> Therefore let all Israel be assured of this: God has made this Jesus, whom you crucified, both Lord and Christ.
> (*Injil*, Acts 2:36 – where 'Lord' is a divine title)

'Ubaydullah, whom we met in chapter 1, was able to accept this assurance. He could see that believing in Jesus the Messiah was not a matter of reverting to paganism. This is true too for Yahya, a British-born Pakistani. As a young man he came to realize that the God his family had worshipped for generations was neither personal nor involved in the world. From Christian friends he discovered that God had a plan of salvation and that this needed to be enacted by God himself in a physical human body. Yahya now knows that God has not left him to try to sort out sin on his own or to work his way to paradise, but has come down to earth to rescue him for paradise. Even when Yahya's best friend died recently (this was the person who had most helped him to see that Jesus is the Word in a human body), he knew that he didn't need to grieve as much as other people do. This was because Jesus took on a mortal body so that he and his friend would one day receive immortal bodies and live with God in a place that can never spoil or fade.

Key points

- The God of the Bible has come down to be with his people at various times.
- As the Word in flesh he did so supremely in Jesus Christ, the 'greater Adam'.
- Because he came to earth, we can see what God is truly like and can be saved from death.

Some questions

For followers of Jesus the Messiah

- What reasons does John 1:14–18 give for the Word becoming a human being?
- Why is it marvellous that our God came to earth?
- The Word gave up his heavenly splendour for our salvation (Philippians 2:5–11). How could you serve your Muslim friends and give up your comforts so that they can hear about this salvation?

For Muslim friends

- How could God be true to his word when he said that humans should rule the world and also that sin should be punished with death?
- Without Jesus as our mediator, how else can death be defeated?
- What certainty do you have of God's presence and a resurrected life?

5. But don't Christians worship three Gods?

The personal and united God

Illogical maths?

In one small corner of London's Hyde Park, people gather to hear all kinds of serious and silly speakers present their ideas, ideologies and solutions to the world's problems. Recently, one of my favourite speakers has been a big Afro-Caribbean guy. He stands on his soapbox dressed in a silky red devil's costume and booms out various random questions to annoy passers-by.

Speakers' Corner apparently became a 'sacred space' for free speech during the nineteenth century as people agitated for political reform in the UK. Socialists, in particular, often had to give their speeches there because they were excluded from other venues. While there is still much political discussion, on Sunday afternoons the debate emphasizes religion. In particular, Christians and Muslims stand on their boxes or stepladders to present their ideas and competing truth-claims. I am not quite sure what all the tourists make of it, but the regulars seem to enjoy the banter and debate.

One time when I was there (not on a soapbox, but just in the crowd), I got chatting to a Muslim guy. Without much introduction, he launched into an attack on the Trinity. 'You say you believe in one God, but then you say Father is God, Jesus is God and Spirit is God. One plus one plus one equals three, not one! How can there be more than one God anyway? They would all argue with each other! The idea of "Trinity" is illogical and was made up by Christians. The word isn't even in the Bible.'

One of the real problems with Speakers' Corner is that this can be the standard of conversation. People are so hyped up about their own views that they reel off their objections to others' opinions without ever seeking an answer or even listening properly. However, these questions and objections are not found only at Speakers' Corner.

Many of my Bengali friends in East London have said similar things, although rarely in one breath or without pausing to listen! The root of these objections is within the Qur'an. Christians are urged not to say 'Three' because God is one God (Surah 4:171). The Qur'an recognizes that the Christian concept of God is linked in some way to the claim that Jesus is the Son of God. It asserts that this idea causes cosmic confusion:

No son did Allah beget, nor is there any god along with Him: (if there were many gods), behold, each god would have taken away what he had created and lorded it over the others!
(Surah 23:91)

When Muslim friends object that Christians are not really being monotheists, we could answer by saying that divine maths is not about addition but multiplication: $1 \times 1 \times 1 = 1$.

We could answer the objection about logic by saying that God is beyond our understanding and is a mystery. Both our religions are founded on convictions about revelation, not logic per se. When they object that the word 'Trinity' isn't found in the Bible, we could respond by saying that the word *Tawhid* (God's oneness) isn't found in the Qur'an, yet both concepts are taught by these books. We could also say that the Qur'an doesn't properly confront the true biblical Trinity because what it condemns is actually the worship of God, Mary and Jesus (Surah 5:73, 75, 116). However, while all these answers are true, we can say much more that is wonderful about our one God who is three persons.

There is one true God and he is to be loved

We must be clear that we do not believe in three gods,[1] just as Jesus was clear.

> One of the teachers of the law came and heard them debating. Noticing that Jesus had given them a good answer, he asked him, 'Of all the commandments, which is the most important?'
>
> 'The most important one,' answered Jesus, 'is this: "Hear, O Israel, the Lord our God, the Lord is one. Love the Lord your God with all your heart and with all your soul and with all your mind and with all your strength." The second is this: "Love your neighbour as yourself." There is no commandment greater than these.'
> (*Injil*, Mark 12:28–31)

Jesus quotes the prophet Moses here (Deuteronomy 6:4–5). This truth about God was not merely to be verbally repeated, but was to be acted upon by loving God wholeheartedly. After all,

> You believe that there is one God. Good! Even the demons
> believe that – and shudder.
> (*Injil*, James 2:19)

Unlike the demons, we are to apply the truth that God is one
by loving the one true God with all of our hearts, souls, minds
and strength.

This response also begins to help us see what it means when
we say God is one. If it simply meant that God is a monad – a
single, indivisible being on his own, as Muslim people believe
– that would not make sense: 'Hear, O Israel, the LORD your
God is a monad; love him.' Why should we love God? Because
he has no-one to love and needs our love? That almost seems
to be implied by my Muslim friends. Therefore, as we have
done before, we need to see what the first prophets said about
God in order to understand what God's oneness means and
why it makes sense to love him.

God in the Old Testament is one because he is the unique . . .

The key way in which the Bible talks of God as one is that the
LORD is God *alone*. As with all words, it is their context which
helps to explain their meaning. In discussing God's oneness
in Deuteronomy, the prophet Moses emphasizes God's uniqueness and incomparability.[2] He alone is to be worshipped, not
any other gods.

My daughter visited a synagogue recently as part of her
religious education curriculum. As the Jewish leaders told
her class about their building and religion, they mentioned
this verse in Deuteronomy about God's oneness. One of the
leaders made the point that it is all about worshipping
God alone, not our idols. The LORD who is one in Deuteronomy 6 is one because he is unique and beyond compare

throughout Deuteronomy and the rest of the Scriptures (see, for example, Deuteronomy 3:24; 4:35, 39; 32:39; Exodus 15:11; Psalm 18:31). At the very least, this shows that our understanding of the Hebrew Scriptures on this particular issue is similar to that of Jewish people.

In many ways, this is like fans at the Emirates Stadium in London shouting, 'There's only one Arsenal!' There's only one team full of youngsters who can run rings around older men in the Carling Cup. There's only one team who can play total football. There's only one team who can thrash the best in Europe and lose to the worst in England in the same week! They are unique and can't be compared with other teams. There is only one Arsenal.[3]

Obviously, God is not Arsenal (nor should Arsenal be worshipped!), so how is the LORD's oneness expressed? It is not through his footballing style, but through being the unique revealing, rescuing, creating and sustaining God.

. . . Revealer and Rescuer

Again, the context in Deuteronomy helps us to see the ways in which we are to understand that God is one or unique. Moses tells us that the LORD is unique because no other god has spoken like him or rescued people like he did:

> Ask now about the former days, long before your time,
> from the day God created man on the earth; ask from one
> end of the heavens to the other. Has anything so great as this
> ever happened, or has anything like it ever been heard of?
> Has any other people heard the voice of God speaking out of
> fire, as you have, and lived? Has any god ever tried to take for
> himself one nation out of another nation, by testings, by
> miraculous signs and wonders, by war, by a mighty hand and
> an outstretched arm, or by great and awesome deeds, like all

the things the LORD your God did for you in Egypt before your very eyes?

You were shown these things so that you might know that the LORD is God; besides him there is no other.

(*Taurat*, Deuteronomy 4:32–35)

. . . Creator and Sustainer

The prophet Isaiah also preaches this uniqueness to God's people. God is incomparable as the Creator and Sustainer of all the earth:

To whom, then, will you compare God?
    What image will you compare him to?
As for an idol, a craftsman casts it,
    and a goldsmith overlays it with gold
    and fashions silver chains for it.
A man too poor to present such an offering
    selects wood that will not rot.
He looks for a skilled craftsman
    to set up an idol that will not topple . . .

To whom will you compare me?
    Or who is my equal? says the Holy One.
Lift your eyes and look to the heavens:
    Who created all these?
He who brings out the starry host one by one,
    and calls them each by name.
Because of his great power and mighty strength,
    not one of them is missing.

(Prophet Isaiah 40:18–20, 25–26)

The nations and their idols are nothing to the one true LORD God. We have seen that very vividly in recent years as the gods of capitalism have come tumbling down. Serving ever-increasing wealth is just like making a dumb idol. It will not meet our needs. Nothing which is made with our own hands or minds can do this. The LORD is incomparable because he is the Creator and Sustainer of all things.

Therefore, to break with biblical monotheism is to think that there is another god worthy of worship or our love. We deny biblical monotheism if we trust in created things, not the uncreated, sole Ruler, Revealer, Rescuer, Creator and Sustainer of the universe.

God in the Old Testament is a deep unity

As we saw in the last chapter, God in the Old Testament surprises us by stepping into his world. Similarly, God surprises us with the depth of his oneness. For example:

> In the beginning God created the heavens and the earth. Now the earth was formless and empty, darkness was over the surface of the deep, and the Spirit of God was hovering over the waters.
>
> And God said, 'Let there be light,' and there was light.
> (*Taurat*, Genesis 1:1–3)

Notice here that we have 'God' and 'the Spirit of God'. We also have God's word acting creatively. God speaks and things happen. This shows that God's word is in itself powerful and life-giving. Therefore, right at the beginning of the Bible, we are introduced to the one true God who is a deep unity: he has a Spirit distinct from him and a word which is powerfully creative in its own right; yet God is still one, unique and worthy of worship alone.

Also, the Old Testament talks about a person called the angel or messenger of the LORD. Sometimes the messenger is

distinct from God and at other times he is called God or LORD
(Genesis 16:9–13; Exodus 3:2–6; 23:20–22; Judges 2:1–2; 6:11,
14). These texts all suggest that more than one person can be
called 'LORD'.

Furthermore, the Psalms describe a divine King who will
come and rule (Psalms 45:6–7; 110:1).[4] The prophet Isaiah
provides more details as he looks forward to the birth, by a
virgin, of the promised King who will be called 'mighty God'
(Isaiah 9:6–7).

Biblical monotheism is not about mathematics but uniqueness, incomparability and depth. At an interfaith dialogue
event I attended, a Jewish rabbi was happy to agree with this.
While he did not believe in the Trinity (because he was not
convinced about Jesus' claims), he did agree that the monotheism of the Hebrew Scriptures was not about oneness in a
mathematical sense. Therefore, having been given our mono-
theistic building blocks in the Old Testament, we can now
turn to the New Testament to see how we should fit them
together.

God in the New Testament is three perfect persons in perfect unity

In the last chapter we looked at the introduction to John's
Gospel, but it is worth quoting in part again:

> The Word [of God] became flesh and made his dwelling
> among us . . .
>   No-one has ever seen God, but God the One and Only,
> who is at the Father's side, has made him known.
> (*Injil*, John 1:14, 18)

The Word of God which we saw at the beginning of creation
is revealed here as a person, distinct from the Father.[5] The

Word of God came into his world to show us truly who God is. Does this mean that there are two gods, each vying for control over the world?

No, although this was what some of Jesus' first hearers thought (John 5).[6] One Sabbath, Jesus healed a paralysed man. This provoked an angry response from some Jewish people. They argued that when Jesus healed the man he had broken the Sabbath because healing was work (the Sabbath is one day out of the week when Jewish people are to rest from work). Jesus responded:

> My Father is always at his work to this very day, and I, too, am working.
> (*Injil*, John 5:17)

This reply only inflamed the situation further:

> For this reason the Jews tried all the harder to kill him; not only was he breaking the Sabbath, but he was even calling God his own Father, making himself equal with God.
> (*Injil*, John 5:18)

The Jews heard Jesus claiming to be a rival to the one true God, the LORD of Moses and the other prophets. (At this point, it's interesting to note that both those who followed Jesus and those who were against him agreed on one thing: Jesus claimed to be divine. This should put to rest any erroneous notion that Jesus never claimed to be divine.) Jesus' reply needed to show that he had not made himself equal with God and wasn't a rival to God:

> Jesus gave them this answer: 'I tell you the truth, the Son can do nothing by himself; he can do only what he sees his

Father doing, because whatever the Father does the Son also does. For the Father loves the Son and shows him all he does. Yes, to your amazement he will show him even greater things than these. For just as the Father raises the dead and gives them life, even so the Son gives life to whom he is pleased to give it. Moreover, the Father judges no-one, but has entrusted all judgment to the Son, that all may honour the Son just as they honour the Father. He who does not honour the Son does not honour the Father, who sent him.

'I tell you the truth, whoever hears my word and believes him who sent me has eternal life and will not be condemned; he has crossed over from death to life. I tell you the truth, a time is coming and has now come when the dead will hear the voice of the Son of God and those who hear will live. For as the Father has life in himself, so he has granted the Son to have life in himself. And he has given him authority to judge because he is the Son of Man.'

(*Injil*, John 5:19–27)

Jesus works inseparably with his Father

Jesus tells us that the Word or Son of God can do nothing by himself. He works inseparably with his Father, which means that they are not two gods – they are two persons perfectly united in their actions. They work together in every action so that the Son only does what the Father shows him. Indeed, the Son works for his Father's glory and honour, not for anyone else's.

Later on in John's Gospel we see that the Father and Son not only work inseparably together, but they are also permanently present in one another (along with the Holy Spirit). For example, Jesus says:

Do not believe me unless I do what my Father does. But if I do it, even though you do not believe me, believe the miracles, that you may know and understand that the Father is in me, and I in the Father.

(*Injil*, John 10:37–38; see also John 14:16–27; 15:26; 16:14–15)

Therefore they are not rivals at all. Instead, they are united in purpose and action. Jesus answers the 'rival' charge by claiming 'inseparable operation'. He works with his Father. The Qur'anic objection that one divine being would lord it over another is unfounded. However, all this talk about Jesus doing nothing by himself opens other possibilities: is he not really divine? Has he made himself God?

Jesus has eternal divine life in himself

To make himself doubly clear that his works came about through being divine and that he had not made himself divine, Jesus said:

For as the Father has life in himself, so he has granted the Son to have life in himself.

(*Injil*, John 5:26)

The Son has exactly the same life in himself as the Father. Just as the Father's life is eternal, so is the Son's. Just as the Father's life is uncreated, so is the Son's. Just as the Father's life is self-sufficient, so is the Son's.

Just as I share the same kind of life as my earthly father, so does the Word of God with his Father. Just as I have the same kind of human nature as my father, so does the Son have the same divine nature as his Father. However, analogies are never completely accurate in all respects, whether they involve Arsenal and God, or human parents and God.

Even if I have the same kind of life as my father, my life began at a point in time. This was not true for the Word of God. His life had no beginning because he has the same life in himself as his eternal Father. The Son of God is eternal and has always been with the Father.

Yet the analogy of father and son is helpful in other ways in understanding God and Jesus. Jesus does act like a true son. He doesn't usurp his Father, but loves and serves him in all that he does. Rather than undermining the oneness of God, the Father–Son relationship actually affirms their unity. Any claims about rivalry and divinity are answered by the facts that Jesus' life is the same as his Father's and Jesus is the Son. Therefore the Father and Son, along with the Holy Spirit, are the completely united, unique, incomparable, revealing, rescuing, creating, one God.

As one would expect, there is no complete analogy in creation by which we can understand this God who is one in three persons. However, the Bible's view of marriage does go some way in giving a picture of how this can happen. A husband and wife are two persons that 'become one flesh' (Genesis 2:24). They remain as two distinct people, but are one united, unique, other-centred marriage unit.

Jesus' divine claims have evidence

To help the Jewish people around him be convinced of these truths, Jesus provided testimonies from John the Baptist, his own miracles and the Old Testament (John 5:31–47). We also need to help our Muslim friends see how these different witnesses point to Jesus, showing him to be truly divine and no rival to God. If the prophet John the Baptist was there to point people to Jesus, surely Jesus must be more than yet another prophet. If Jesus the Messiah brings life and has power over nature, surely this shows him doing the same things as the God of the Old Testament. If diligent study of the Scriptures shows that a promised divine King is coming, surely we should take seriously someone who claims to be that King.

If Jesus is who he claimed to be, he has not broken with biblical monotheism nor have his followers. Just to remind ourselves, we deny biblical monotheism if we trust in created things, but Jesus is uncreated and has the same ruling, revealing, rescuing, creating and sustaining powers as his Father. Therefore we can say that they are one God (with the Holy Spirit).

Value and relationship from the personal triune God

Our Western culture often treats people as interchangeable individuals. We can be viewed as clones whose differences don't really matter: I'm just another voter for David, Ed or Nick, or just another consumer at Asda, Sainsbury's or Tesco. Neither David nor Asda cares who I am; all they care about is that I choose them.

When I used to work in the civil service, my colleagues and I were called by our pay bands. For example, 'Pay Band 3s need to meet in such-and-such a place to discuss such-and-such a piece of red tape.' We were also treated interchangeably. There was a general idea that anyone in a particular pay band could do the work of someone else in their pay band (however different that work was). One absurd example I experienced was this: a Pay Band 4 man (who was normally responsible for looking after our buildings) was expected to provide legal advice to Pay Band 3 case officers dealing with enquiries from charities – just because *other* Pay Band 4 people were able to give legal advice! Such attitudes demean people. They can also cause employees to have feelings of low self-esteem and high insecurity.

Yet the fact that there is one God in three persons means that individual difference is important. Individuality is right at the heart of the universe. Like the Father, Son and Spirit, each of us is unique because we are made in their image. Therefore, if we are feeling that our identity is tied to our voting record or consumer preferences or pay grade, we should look to God. He values us as different, distinct people.

In case we go too far along this track and into self-centred individualism, the triune God of the Bible again challenges us. We might have *i*Pods, *i*Phones, *My* Documents and *My*Space, but our one God in three persons means that relationships are fundamental. There is more than 'I' and 'my'. We are made to relate to others. More than this, such relationships should be other-centred. Just as the Father loves the Son and shows him all he does, the Son seeks to honour the Father in obedience. The Father and Son are other-centred, as is the Spirit who glorifies the Son.

Therefore there is no basis for demonizing or de-humanizing people. There is no 'other'. All are human beings because all are made in God's image. Therefore all are valued and should be served. Indeed this must be why, in the verses quoted at the beginning of this chapter, Jesus followed up his command to 'love God' with a command to 'love your neighbour'.

Allah's denial of choice

Our understanding of Ultimate Reality leads us to mould the world to fit that Reality. Within Islam, it appears that the oneness or *Tawhid* of God means that all individuals must be subsumed into one. If God is impersonal and undifferentiated, then it is likely that his followers will be as well.

As I relate to my Muslim friends in the East End this is what I see. Many of them feel compelled to wear the same Arab clothes to be devout, to have the same long beards (for men), to wear the same *hijab* (for women, while their mothers wear the Bengali *shalwar kameez* instead) and not to have different views on issues. This is not to say that all Muslim people act the same way, but that those who are seeking to be more devout do begin to reject their previous cultural symbols or outward differences and to develop an outward uniformity.

When asked about this, the men often say that they are following Muhammad's example (as expressed in Surah 33:21) while the women say they are following his wives'. This example is not just in actions or attitudes, but also in outward appearances. I have been to a number of talks put on by university Islamic societies where the speaker has challenged the male Muslims there to follow in Muhammad's footsteps by dressing like him and having a beard like him.[7]

As Muhammad took power in Medina, and Islam spread across the Middle East and the Mediterranean, there was an imposition of Islam from the top down. This is not to say that people were given the choice to 'convert or die', but that the goal of Muhammad's followers was to achieve state power, and the community beneath the state had to submit to their rule (much like the European colonial movement of the nineteenth to twentieth centuries). However, we do see more explicit coercion in the attitude to those who leave Islam.

An individual's personal choice to reject Islam for another creed is a threat to the oneness of Muslim people and therefore must be stopped.[8] An individual's access to other choices may also be limited; for example, the governments in Afghanistan, Egypt, Indonesia, Kuwait, Saudi Arabia, Syria, Tajikistan, Turkey, Turkmenistan, Uzbekistan and Yemen prohibit other religions from openly proclaiming their faith.

I realize that this sounds negative, but Islam seems unwilling to allow people to act as distinct persons, whether or not they are Muslim. It seems to compel people to be the same. However, if God is God, he does not need to coerce people or make them all the same.

The triune God is the answer . . .

. . . for society

God, as revealed in the Bible, provides the antidote to both rigid conformity and selfish individualism. The one true God is a community of persons. Just as God is truly God by being Father, Son and Spirit relating to one another, so it is in relating to other people that human beings are truly human. Such true humans can also be part of a true community where both unity and diversity are celebrated. This doesn't mean that a nation should be made up of diverse communities living in their own spaces and never engaging with one another (though our politicians might suggest this); it means one united community of different, other-centred people who serve each other.[9]

As the French social anthropologist Maurice Godelier has written, 'Human beings, in contrast to other social animals, do not just live in society, they produce society in order to live.'[10] Although I disagree with Godelier's Marxist presuppositions, he is right in his analysis because we are made in the image of our personal, social God. His imprint is on us as persons. This is why we make societies.

We see within the Godhead that the Father loves the Son and shows him all he does. He gives the Son a wonderful inheritance and sends the Son to fulfil the vision of a new creation. The Son obeys the Father even to the point of dying. In his resurrection, ascension and return he gives all honour to his Father. The Holy Spirit is sent by the Father and the Son to bring people into the Son's new creation. The Spirit makes the Son known among the nations and lives in people so that their lives are God-honouring, selfless and just.

Within the Godhead, therefore, the Father, Son and Spirit live in joyful, righteous, self-giving, other-enriching intimacy.

Imagine if our marriages, our families and our communities were marked by such love. What a difference that would make! Having been made in God's image, we were made for such a life.

. . . for salvation

The Christian belief that God exists in three persons (this chapter) and that one of these persons took on a physical body to be with his people (the previous chapter) comes together even more tightly when we realize, with amazement, that this concerns our salvation as well. Rather than repeat various Bible verses given already, here is an illustration which might help us to rejoice in these truths:

> One day Ahmad fell into a hole in the desert. He was stuck until a face appeared at the top and said, 'I am alone but I will send down a book so you can work out how to rescue yourself.' Ahmad spent the rest of his life trying to climb out of the hole on his own but without success.
>
> The next day Mabrouk fell into another hole in the desert. This time three faces appeared at the top of the hole. The first (the brave one) said, 'I'll go down if someone else (the strong one) will hold the rope for me.' The third (the gentle one) said, 'While you are doing that I'll encourage you both.' So the brave one went down and saved Mabrouk. However, while he was doing so, the hole collapsed and buried the brave one, killing him. The strong one dug and dug for three days to get him out. Meanwhile the gentle one came down the hole too and breathed life back into the brave one and he lived again.[11]

As with all analogies, we don't want to push all the details, but it leaves us with a big question: which would you rather have, a book or a personal rescue team to save you?

Eternally loving?

As a result of the booktable mentioned at the beginning of chapter 4, I got to know an imam. He had been emotionally scarred by Christians in the past, but he started to come to our church to see what kind of Christians we were. I met with him a couple of times, for coffee, to study the Bible and Qur'an together, and simply to try to build bridges. One time, we talked about the nature of God and he said that he was happy to call God 'Father'. He also took comfort from knowing that this Father was loving towards him. However, such comfort is essentially without foundation.

This is because Muslim people's God is not eternally Father nor eternally loving. If God is on his own (before the creation of the universe), then he has no-one to be father to or to love. Both of these ideas require an object for them to be true. A father has to have a child to be a father. A lover has to have a beloved in order to love. Therefore love and fatherhood are not essential to God in himself. They are later additions. In himself, from eternity, God is neither relational nor loving. God is neither essentially nor eternally loving. The imam could see my logic, but did not like its logical conclusion. The Bible, on the other hand, is clear that God is love, was love eternally and will be love forever.

Key points

- We believe in one, unique, incomparable and loving God who is three persons working together in perfect unity.
- We come to know God through the Son revealing the Father and Spirit to us.
- Such knowledge frees us from individualism and totalitarianism.

Some questions

For followers of Jesus the Messiah

- Why is it wonderful that the God of the Bible is three persons?
- How does the fact that the universe's Ultimate Reality is Father, Son and Spirit help us not to be self-absorbed?
- What Bible passages could you take a Muslim friend to if he or she said, 'The Trinity isn't in the Bible'?

For Muslim friends

- Within Islam, to what extent do people and relationships matter? Why?
- Within Islam, are people simply interchangeable with others? Why / Why not?
- If God is not personal or loving in himself and from all eternity, why did he create personal beings? Can he love or communicate with them?

6. Where does Christianity end and Western culture begin?

The multicultural gospel

Bunnies and piggies

A couple of years ago, Asad and I shared a platform at one of the London universities to talk about the 'reasonableness' of our faith. Asad's idea was to show secularists that we could reason with one another and explain how our respective faiths had reasonable foundations. This was to challenge the ideology of atheists who assert that people of faith are irrational and dangerous.

The lecture theatre was pretty full, with a mixture of atheists, Christians and Muslims as we had hoped. Unfortunately, most of the questions in the Questions and Answers session seemed directed at me, as Christians often seem too polite to ask searching things of a Muslim speaker. After trying to answer people's queries for an hour or so, we came to an end and I could breathe a sigh of relief (until I had to review it all before it went up on YouTube and more people could assess our reasonableness!). As I was preparing to go, a Muslim student came up to me and asked, 'I hope this doesn't sound too silly,

but where do Easter bunnies come from? Are they in the Bible?'
This particular event took place just after Easter, so in many
ways it was a reasonable question. However, it also highlighted
a certain amount of confusion in the questioner's mind.

One Pakistani-background family we had the pleasure of
hosting at our house had a different question: 'Why, when we
have so much in common, do you eat pork?' A Bengali friend
made a similar point to my wife: 'Why, when you are respect-
able and modest, don't you cover your head like me?' And
another friend asked, 'Why do you have Christmas trees in
your house, when they're a pagan symbol?' (Many Bengali
people also believe that trees contain evil spirits and so they
refuse to walk in the woods and think it's dangerous to bring
a tree into your home.)

Two broad themes emerge from these different questions.
First, the problem of cultural symbols: many Muslim people
are confusing the symbols attached to particular festivals (such
as Easter bunnies and Christmas trees) with biblical Christianity.
Second, the question of outward practices: Western Christians
don't tend to adhere to rules about food, drink and clothing,
unlike in Islam.

The second issue is further complicated by the fact that
some Christians across the world today do have such outward
practices, as did other Christians in the past. Does our lack of
them here and now mean that many Christians living in
twenty-first-century Britain aren't truly biblical? Are we not
living lives which are pleasing to God?

This is certainly what many Muslim people think. Hopefully
chapter 2 has shown that Christian people do try to live good
lives here and now. However, another part of the answer is
through understanding that the good news of Jesus is both
for all time and also for all peoples and is not tied to one
particular cultural expression.

The Bible challenges every culture

The Bible doesn't agree with the thinking or lifestyle of any one particular culture. It confronts and challenges everyone. Therefore it isn't tied to one culture nor is it from one culture (in fact it must come from outside human culture, as I argue in the next chapter).[1]

For example, the Bible teaches us that we should love our enemies (Luke 6:27–36) and that sex should be within heterosexual monogamous marriage (Genesis 2:22–24; Exodus 20:14; 1 Corinthians 6:9–20). In general terms, Westerners like the first bit about loving our enemies, but reject the sex bit. Easterners, on the other hand, usually like the bit about marriage, but reject the love for enemies. Therefore, in general terms, these teachings could not have been made up by either Western or Eastern culture.

The Bible affirms culture

From the very beginning of humanity's creation, God commanded people to spread across the earth and rule over it (Genesis 1:26–30). As creatures made in his image, people were to be God's representatives on the earth and therefore their rule was not to be exploitative. Instead they were to be good and work to bring about good in the world so that it was a good place for all of humanity to live under God. While the 'fall' (Genesis 3) clearly marred this image and meant that humanity's rule was corrupted, Adam and Eve's sin did not negate God's mandate because it was affirmed again to the prophet Noah (Genesis 9:1–7).

Therefore, by Genesis 4 we see people 'doing culture', that is, making and doing things which create the context for their lives and enable life to be lived in this world. Cain grew crops, Abel and Jabal kept flocks of animals, Jubal constructed musical instruments and Tubal-cain made bronze and iron tools. Each of these things could be used for harmful purposes towards other people; for example bronze could be shaped into swords and iron into spears. But equally they could be used for good, perhaps to make farming implements. Musical instruments can lead us to praise our Creator, as is urged in Psalm 150:

Praise the LORD.

Praise God in his sanctuary;
    praise him in his mighty heavens.
Praise him for his acts of power;
    praise him for his surpassing greatness.
Praise him with the sounding of the trumpet,
    praise him with the harp and lyre,
praise him with tambourine and dancing,
    praise him with the strings and flute,
praise him with the clash of cymbals,
    praise him with resounding cymbals.

Let everything that has breath praise the LORD.

Praise the LORD.

And yet they can also lead to music which glorifies false gods like humanity, nature, money, sex and power – from Beethoven's Ninth Symphony, *Ode to Joy*, to Abba's 'Mamma Mia'. Cultural artefacts, like music, are neutral in themselves. Although we are marred images of God and therefore can use such things for good or bad purposes, we are not prohibited from making or using them in the first place. The Bible itself affirms not just human artefacts, like tools and instruments, but also cultural differences like the languages we speak, the food we eat, the clothes we wear and the days we celebrate.

Languages

God's actions at the Tower of Babel (Genesis 11:1–9) seem to be both an action of judgment and a speeding-up of his commands to Adam and Eve. Rather than spreading out across the world as God commanded in Genesis 1 and 9, people gathered together to oppose God. Therefore God scattered them across the world and gave them new languages to speak.

As we know, one language may change not only through time, but also across space, even within one country. Someone from Glasgow has a lot in common with a Londoner in terms of language, but they also have differences in accent, dialect and vocabulary. If that can happen naturally across a short distance, it is likely that God's plan for human beings to spread out across the world (Genesis 1) was partly intended to lead to different languages. Therefore, while God did act in judgment at Babel, he also acted in grace by moving people into ways he wanted them to walk in.

This is confirmed when we see what happened with languages in New Testament times. When the apostle Peter stood up in Jerusalem at Pentecost to tell people all about Jesus, he didn't speak in Hebrew or Aramaic; rather, he and the other apostles proclaimed the good news about Jesus in every language represented there (Acts 2). In the new creation, when all God's people from all the different tribes, people-groups and nations will live with him in his perfect paradise, people will be praising God in their own languages – united in praise, diverse in its outworking (Revelation 7:9–12).

In many ways, this is a reflection of who God is. Just as he is one God in three persons, so his people are united yet diverse. God is all the more glorified when he is worshipped by so many people in so many different ways.

The biblical text itself affirms different languages. Its text has always been a translated Word. Adam, Eve and Abraham, for example, are highly unlikely to have spoken the kind of Hebrew we find written down in Genesis. However, God moved the prophet Moses to write down their words and the narratives about them in Hebrew so that Moses' people, who spoke Hebrew, could understand them.

Similarly, while Jesus probably spoke Greek, it is unlikely that he spoke exclusively in the Greek we find in the four Gospels. However, because Greek was the language most widely spoken in the Mediterranean of the first century, God moved the apostles to write down their narratives about Jesus in Greek. This helps us to see that God is concerned to communicate his truth to his people in a language they can understand. It also shows us that the Bible is God's Word in whatever language it's translated into.

Muslim friends sometimes suggest that there are many versions of the Bible, for example the New International Version, the King James Version. However, this is a misunderstanding of the word 'version'. It doesn't mean a new and changed model, as it might with a car, but is a word used instead of 'translation'. I could say that my bookshelf has five or six different versions of the Qur'an, but what I mean is that I have five or six different translations.[2]

The Bible is the very Word of God, living and active, in Arabic, Bengali, English, French, Mandarin, Urdu or whatever else. God wants to communicate with all people everywhere in ways that they can understand so that they can respond and enter his paradise. Therefore it seems unlikely that God would ever limit himself to communicating in one language, whether Hebrew or Greek or Arabic.

Here, as outlined in the last chapter, Islam seems to reflect its own understanding of *Tawhid* or oneness. From the many Arabic courses offered in mosques it's hard not to draw the conclusion that you can understand the Qur'an only by understanding Arabic. It's hard not to think that God doesn't speak my language.

Food

Back in Genesis 1 again, God gave Adam and Eve every plant and fruit tree to eat (verse 29). By the time we come to Noah in Genesis 9, all animals were good for food too (verse 3). God then limited his people to certain types of food after they left Egypt and were given his laws at Mount Sinai (Leviticus 11; Deuteronomy 14). If everything was good to eat, why did God limit their food in this way?

The answer seems to be that food marks out people, and God's people then were to be marked out from the nations around them.[3] Just as some English people call the French 'Frogs' and some French people return the compliment with '*Rosbifs*', so God's people then were to be known as those who did not eat pig and many other types of animal. When God's people were rescued from Egypt, they were not all ethnically or culturally the same, but they were all set apart as God's holy nation (Exodus 12:38; 19:5). They had very little which marked them off from the many pagan nations around them and so God gave them particular 'boundary markers', such as food, to show that they were his treasured possession.

As Jesus Christ came into the world, he fulfilled the Old Testament law as a whole (through his perfect obedience and right interpretation of it, as well as being the perfect sacrifice it pointed to). Part of this fulfilment involved breaking down boundary markers between Jews and non-Jews so that God's people are no longer defined by cultural things, such as food or circumcision, but by faith in Jesus and by living transformed lives (as described in chapter 2). Indeed, the law is also said to lead us to Christ like a teacher. Once you have arrived at Christ you don't need the teacher in quite the same way.[4]

In particular, when it comes to food, Jesus himself declared all food clean (Mark 7:1–23). It isn't what goes into our stomachs that makes us unclean before God. Food just passes through us. Rather, it's what we say and do that defiles us before God. Our thoughts and actions show a defiled heart in need of cleansing. All food created by God is good and can be enjoyed. Therefore we can eat or drink all kinds of food, as long as we do it giving thanks to God and not being mastered by it (1 Corinthians 6:12; 1 Timothy 4:4).

Clothes

A few months ago a female colleague and I were invited to be interviewed on a Shia TV channel. It was a documentary on religious clothing and women, particularly about wearing the veil. Very kindly the interviewer sent us her questions beforehand, which gave us time to prepare.

As part of my preparation I considered the use of the term 'veil' in the Bible. The first Bible reference concerns Rebecca putting on the veil prior to meeting Isaac (Genesis 24:65). This was done as a sign of modesty. The second reference is to Tamar putting on the veil to fool her father-in-law Judah into sleeping with her (Genesis 38:13–16). This was clearly not a sign of modesty. These two examples, like food, show us that our clothing doesn't make us pure or impure. What goes on in our hearts determines purity.

My Muslim friends say that the reason women veil themselves is to protect their own modesty as well as to help men not to be sexually tempted. Part of this seems to come from the Qur'anic idea about Adam and Eve's sin in the Garden.

They were said to have obeyed Satan by uncovering their private parts to one another (Surah 7:10–32). God then provided clothing for the couple to wear outside paradise. Humanity is to learn from this and not let Satan deceive people into exposing themselves (see also Surahs 17:61–64; 20:115–124).

While it is true that Christians should always avoid sexual immorality and not cause others to commit such sin, there is no explicit dress code involved. This is true for both men and women. Also, Christians believe that the human body is not in itself shameful. Adam and Eve's sin in the Garden was more about rebellion against God than impropriety towards one another. (Indeed, sex and our bodies are celebrated within the Bible, when they are placed in the right context of heterosexual, monogamous, lifelong marriage, as King Solomon's Song of Songs makes clear.)

The apostle Paul in one of his letters does say that women should have their heads covered, but this appears to be a cultural symbol of submission to their husbands (1 Corinthians 11:2–16). If women were to speak in church without their heads covered it would be as if they were saying: 'As a Christian I'm so free that I'm no longer married or under my husband's headship.' Therefore the apostle Paul directed these wives to maintain their head coverings. A parallel today would be a situation where wives threw away their wedding rings because of their freedom as Christians. The principle (submission) remains, but the symbol (such as a head covering or a ring) changes across time and cultures.[5]

Therefore, as with freedom about food, we are free to wear what we like, within certain parameters: we shouldn't cause others to sin and we shouldn't rely on outward appearance to make us beautiful. It is the inner beauty of following God which is most important.

Days

A few years ago we regularly helped some Bengali children with their schoolwork. We got to know one another well and became good friends. One week near Christmas, the children didn't have any homework so we had a Christmas quiz. Rather than one based on *Who Wants To Be a Millionaire?* we used the story of the wise men visiting the infant Jesus in Bethlehem (we are Christians, after all!). We did a simple comprehension exercise on the text of Matthew 2:1–12 to see what it says, as well as throwing in the odd random question like 'Did Father Christmas visit Jesus too?' and 'Does verse 1 tell us that Jesus was born on 25 December?'

Of course, the Bible doesn't give us the particular date of the virgin birth; in fact it doesn't say that Christians should celebrate the birth at all, let alone on a particular day. So are we going beyond the Bible by celebrating Jesus' birth? Indeed, if 25 December actually refers to a pagan celebration, doesn't this show us to be hopelessly compromised by our Western culture?

It is true that many of the trappings of Christmas, with all its commercialism and excess, are not Christian. However, this doesn't necessarily mean that Christians are compromised by celebrating on this day.

First, there is no biblical command against celebrating Christmas. If Jesus' birth is as wonderful as I have tried to show already, then it makes sense for us to want to celebrate it and be glad. After all, the angels who announced Jesus' birth said that they brought 'good news of great joy' (Luke 2:10).

Second, as Christians view all cultures through the lens of the Bible, we are free to celebrate the good in any culture and to reject the bad. We are also able to redeem or transform aspects of a culture and to turn them into things which praise

God. Therefore, if there are cultural symbols, artefacts and festivals which we can refocus to help people to celebrate the one true God, then we are free to do so. This can help people see that God is the God of their culture and not a tribal deity or the god of an imperial invader.

So, if ancient Europeans celebrated the idea that on 25 December the sun was not defeated but would return, isn't it suitable to take that date and celebrate the coming of Jesus as promised by the prophet Malachi?

> the sun of righteousness [Jesus] will rise with healing in its wings.
> (Prophet Malachi 4:2)

The same could be true of birthdays. We can celebrate another year of life granted by God and praise him for it. However, as with all aspects of culture, there is a danger that these things can be usurped for wrong purposes or can lead Christians astray.

Therefore we need to constantly re-evaluate whether something can be 'redeemed' or whether it should be ignored. Maybe the way in which Christmas has been re-paganized in the West does mean that it is time for us here to remember Jesus' birth in other ways.

Overriding principles

As believers in Christ, God's people are free to speak whatever language they like, to eat all foods or to be picky, to wear the veil or have an uncovered head, to celebrate Christmas or to ignore it. Many Muslim friends find this confusing. It can also be a confusing freedom for Christian believers from a Muslim background: 'Where are the rules for life? It seems like you make it up as you go along!'

Christians have principles and freedom. Our principles are derived through discerning how God reveals his will progressively from the time of creation, through the fall, into the period of ancient Israel, and then centring on Jesus as the fulfilment of God's plans and moving on into the new creation. As God's treasured possession, we try to live good lives, but such good lives will vary in their detail across space and time. Different Christians can live for God in their own cultural way so that he is praised by all different kinds of people in all different kinds of ways.

The apostle Paul explained this most clearly in 1 Corinthians 8:1 – 11:1, when he wanted to help Christians to live in the pagan culture at Corinth, a major city in Greece. Paul advised them to steer a course between joining in the idolatry of the temple culture and being so separated from it that pagans would never get to know any Christians and so never hear about Jesus. The overriding principle is that Christians should live for God's glory as they try to enable as many people as possible to be saved. So this might mean that:

- a Nigerian Christian woman wears masses of colourful material on her head, while an English woman has her head covered by her brown hair;
- a Pakistani believer from a Muslim background neither eats pork sausages nor drinks alcohol, while a Scotsman enjoys his bacon and beer;
- a Korean missionary learns Bengali to explain the Christian message to people in Bangladesh in their own language, while a Korean Christian in Seoul speaks in Korean to her Buddhist colleague about Jesus;
- a seventeenth-century Puritan Christian in England refuses to celebrate Christmas because it is a time for

immoral behaviour, while Christians in twenty-first-century England make the most of 'Nine Lessons and Carols' to present the Christian message in a culturally appropriate way to unbelievers.

The important thing to note is that all these different Christians are working out how the Bible's principles apply to their particular cultural context, so that they can best glorify God and not cause people to be offended by anything except the good news of Jesus.

Back to bunnies and piggies

For the Muslim friends who began this discussion, it's important that we help them see how the many cultural symbols around them are not necessarily tied to the Bible and its principles. Easter bunnies are not biblical, but we're free to enjoy the chocolate eggs they bring(?!), or not to as the case may be. We must help our Muslim friends see that there is a distinction between Western culture and Christianity. In this regard, it may well be that our friends provide a helpful critique, showing where the church in our nation has become too close to our culture. It might be the case that our churches need to participate less in the materialistic culture around us and totally reject its idols.

When it comes to Christmas trees, for example, we might feel that these bring too much identification with the com-mercialism of Christmas and so decide not to have them. Or we might not have a tree because some Muslim people have the impression that we're worshipping it. Or then again we might have one so that any of our friends and family who are atheists will feel at home when they visit us on Christmas Day. Or we might have one to help our Bengali friends see that we don't fear any tree-spirits. (For these people in particular, we again have an opportunity to help them see how Jesus has conquered all evil powers.)

We might also need to help our Muslim friends to see why we don't have to adhere to many of the outward practices of Islam which have an appearance of religiosity and devotion to God. Many of these practices are similar to those in the law of Moses. To keep to them as a way of pleasing God is to miss the fact that such law should lead us to Christ. Not eating or drinking certain things is a backward step in terms of God's progressive revelation. (We may not want to eat or drink for other reasons, such as not causing offence to the people we are with, but not because God says that we must not consume these things.) As with the question of whether people should be circumcised or not, what really counts is keeping God's commands, expressing our faith through love, and living as a new creation.[6] The friends I mentioned in the first couple of paragraphs of this chapter can hopefully see this in our lives, as we try to live for God by loving him and doing good.

There are many other cultural and contextual issues which we could think about here, but there is just not the space, unfortunately. However, the Bible gives us all that we need in order to engage with, embrace and critique culture. It is to the Bible's sufficiency and authority that we now turn.

Key points

- As people made in God's image we are to engage in God's world.
- As Christian people we are free to embrace and critique culture depending on whether it accords with or is against God's Word.

- Although external things do matter and should be done for God's glory, these will vary; what truly matters is having our hearts clean before God.

Some questions

For followers of Jesus the Messiah

- What things in your life are too similar to sinful aspects of our culture and are not Christian enough?
- In what ways could you take on other people's culture so that they could hear about Jesus?
- What things would you be willing to give up in order to help your Muslim friends to hear about Jesus?

For Muslim friends

- What do you think about the idea that God communicates in all human languages?
- Do you recognize that no one culture can be identified as 'Christian'?
- Why would you go back to a law which Jesus has fulfilled?

7. Hasn't the Bible been corrupted?

The trustworthiness of God's living and powerful Word

Introduction

Imran had asked me to speak at a community centre he runs in East London. Every week a group of guys meet to discuss the weather, poetry, sport, politics, religion and anything else which takes their fancy. The guys have all sorts of backgrounds – Christian, Muslim, Hindu, atheist, white British, South Asian British, Afro-Caribbean – a real Diversity Tsar's dream! Once a month, the discussion focuses on differences and similarities between Christianity and Islam. I was asked to give the Christian perspective on the topic of the 'Revelation of God'.

After a great curry, the group of twenty-five men moved onto sofas to hear the two speakers and grill them with their questions. It was a good atmosphere and no-one asked their questions in order to show off or to put down someone else. One question particularly stayed with me: 'Robert, you've said so much I can agree with about God and his Word, so why don't you accept the Qur'an?'

It's a good question. In many ways it's answered by the thread which runs through this book – the Bible is God's story of bringing people back to himself, and Jesus is the centre and fulfilment of that story. Therefore I don't need anyone beyond Jesus the Messiah nor any book beyond the Bible. This obviously raises questions of where the Qur'an does or does not fit in.

The Qur'an and the previous Scriptures: part 1

Muhammad seems to have had similar questions in his mind too. Much of the time, the Qur'an seems to show that it is in keeping with the Bible and that Muhammad is a prophet like the other biblical prophets. In Surahs 2:67–96 and 7:103–171, for example, the text intends to draw a parallel between Muhammad's dealings with the Jews in Medina and Moses' experience with Israel in the wilderness. The Qur'an also tries to show how it is confirming the message as revealed in the previous Scriptures (Surahs 6:92; 10:37; 46:12).

On the other hand, the Qur'an also alleges that Jewish people have in some way altered the Scriptures' words. Surah 2:75 says that Jewish people heard the word of Allah and then knowingly perverted it. Surahs 4:46 and 5:41 say that they displaced words from their right places. Surah 5:13 asserts that Jewish hearts grew hard, such that they changed words from their right place and forgot a good part of the message. Before we say that the Qur'an is contradicting itself here, both confirming the previous Scriptures and alleging their alteration, is there a way of integrating these different verses?

I think there is. The simplest and most obvious way is to say that the Jewish people who were alleged to have altered Scripture were not actually rewriting what was in the Law and the Prophets but were misquoting or misapplying it or misreading the context. Indeed, this is how Yusuf Ali seems to understand these verses.[1]

Also, Muhammad himself seems to hold the book of Moses in high regard and to read from it, as Ibn Kathir, an eighth-century Muslim scholar, tells us in his commentary on the Qur'an:[2]

> Abu Dawud recorded that Ibn 'Umar said, 'Some Jews came to the Messenger of Allah and invited him to go to the Quff area. So he went to the house of Al-Midras and they said, "O Abu Al-Qasim! A man from us committed adultery with a woman, so decide on their matter." They arranged a pillow for the Messenger of Allah and he sat on it and said, "Bring the Tawrah to me." He was brought the Tawrah and he removed the pillow from under him and placed the Tawrah on it, saying, "I trust you and He Who revealed it to you."'[3]

Muhammad respected, read and listened to the *Tawrah* or *Taurat* of Moses. He did not think that it had been changed. Indeed, if Muhammad respected the *Taurat* this means that he should also have respected the concepts of a personal, promise-making God (chapter 1) and a sacrifice for sin (chapter 3), as these are recorded in the *Taurat*. However, after Muhammad died and as Muslim people increasingly began to read the Bible and the Qur'an, they found that they said different things on crucial matters such as who God is and how someone can get to paradise. Therefore, there arose the accusation that the Bible had been corrupted.[4]

As I mentioned in the introduction, many of the other objections to the Christian faith can be gleaned from the Qur'an. This one, concerning the truthfulness of the Christian Scriptures, cannot. This chapter takes a number of approaches to help us see why the Bible is completely trustworthy and sufficient for living our lives under God.

A historical parallel

Back in 1996–1997 I was working for the social development programmes of the Church of Bangladesh. I was based mainly in Old Dhaka, but I was also involved in community projects around the country. I was working there when Bangladesh celebrated the twenty-fifth anniversary of Victory Day. It was very moving.

The event commemorated the time when Bangladesh threw out an imperial power. We remembered the many people who died so that Bangladesh might be free. Possibly more than 1 million people died to enable the country of Bangla-speakers[5] to become a nation in its own right and gain its independence.

That first Victory Day was nearly forty years ago as I write.[6] This was before I was born and before the lifetime of many of my Bengali friends too. It is history, yet it is still fresh in the minds of many older people. Our younger minds can know about it, be appalled by it and be inspired by it through the many books or documentaries which have been produced. Eyewitnesses to these resources and the events themselves abound and so we can also talk to these people in order to back up or refute what we read or watch.

Interestingly, this lapse of time between the events in Bangladesh and ourselves is a slightly greater time-lapse than that between the events of Jesus the Messiah's life, death and resurrection and most of the first writings about him. Just as there are eyewitnesses alive today to authenticate the writings about Victory Day, so there were many eyewitnesses alive when the accounts and analyses of Jesus the Messiah's life, death and resurrection were written. We will come back to the implications of this nearer the end, but for now I want us simply to realize that we are as close to the first Victory Day as the original readers of the New Testament or *Injil* were to the first Resurrection Day.

The Bible is the Book of books

One of the things which can often confuse Muslim people is that the Bible is a collection of books rather than just one book like the Qur'an. Indeed this again highlights one of the barriers Muslim people have to reading the Bible. They come to it with their Islamic presupposition of what a book revealed by God should look like. This is founded on the idea that because the Qur'an was given in a certain way to Muhammad, so the *Taurat* was given to Moses, the *Zabur* to David, and the *Injil* to Jesus. As the Qur'an was dictated by Allah from his Eternal Tablet to Muhammad via the angel Gabriel (Surahs 85:21–22; 96:1–3), so should it be for these other books too. It is really eye-opening for Muslim people to see that this was not how these revelations were given and that the Bible is really a library of God's books.

The earliest biblical books, like Genesis and Exodus, date from the time of the prophet Moses, around the fifteenth century BC. The latest books, like Matthew and Mark, date from the middle of the first century AD. Therefore this Book of books covers a writing period of over 1,500 years.

Despite being written over such a long period of time, by many different authors, there is a clear development of common themes. There is a miraculous unity overall. This commonality and unity suggests an overruling by a divine Author. The divine Author made sure that the human authors wrote down what he wanted them to write. He made sure that they stuck to his script and to his storyline. It is the Book of God's story to God's world.

This helps to explain why there is so much written about the Bible. It helps to explain why it has influenced so many cultures across the world, although it came out of a fairly insignificant corner of the world. This story tells us about God's goodness, humanity's sinfulness and God's gracious promises to bless people from all nations. It culminates in forgiveness being won through Jesus' death and resurrection.

There is no place in this storyline for another book, such as the Qur'an, to be revealed. If Jesus is the centre of God's plans and the New Testament is what we need to see this, we require nothing more. Just as *The Lord of the Rings Trilogy* doesn't need a fourth book to complete it because the evil Sauron has been defeated, or as *Star Wars* doesn't need a seventh film because the Dark Side has been conquered and balance has been brought to the Force, so we don't need any new books to understand God or any new prophets to reveal him to us. Jesus the Messiah has definitively revealed God and conquered evil. The Bible is the ultimate witness to this.

The Bible doesn't promise another ultimate prophet

Although Jesus and others told us that other prophets might arise, whom we are to test to see if they are genuine (for example, Matthew 24; 1 John 4), these are not people who supersede Jesus. For a prophet to be true, he must confirm what Jesus the Messiah has already revealed and achieved.

Muslim people sometimes say that the New Testament promises another prophet to come who will be the ultimate prophet, namely Muhammad. They often try to use passages like John 14:16 to say that this is really a promise about Muhammad. This is where Jesus said:

> And I will ask the Father, and he will give you another
> Counsellor to be with you for ever – the Spirit of truth. The
> world cannot accept him, because it neither sees him nor

knows him. But you know him, for he lives with you and will
be in you.

(*Injil*, John 14:16–17)

Part of the argument made by Muslim people is that the Greek
word translated here as 'Counsellor' is not *paraklete* but *periclyte*
which is a Greek word meaning 'praised one' or 'Ahmad'
(a name for Muhammad in Surah 61:6). Without the need to
get into Greek grammar, we can be clear that there neither is
nor was any Greek text of John's Gospel anywhere in the world
which has the word *periclyte*. It just does not exist.

Furthermore, the context shows that Jesus could not have
been speaking about Muhammad (and so we don't have to
know Greek, fortunately). Jesus was speaking here on the night
before his crucifixion. He was speaking first and foremost to
his eleven disciples (Judas had left by this stage of the evening).
He was preparing them for the events of his death and beyond.
So when Jesus said that the Father would give 'another
Counsellor to be with you for ever' he was primarily promising
this other Counsellor to the Eleven. Muhammad was born 600
years later and could not come to be with the Eleven. Also,
Muhammad didn't live forever nor did he live within Jesus'
followers (as the Counsellor would – explained in verse 17).

Later context shows us that this Counsellor is the Holy
Spirit. This is not to denigrate Muhammad, but just to say that
he is not the focus of these verses. The sending of the Holy
Spirit completes Jesus' rescue mission. We don't need anyone
else to come nor any other book to be given.[7]

The Bible claims to be God's living Word to his world

If God's authorship of the Bible is implied by the fact that it
is one unified narrative, the Bible also explicitly claims that

what its human authors wrote down was from God. For example, Jesus said:

> The Counsellor, the Holy Spirit, whom the Father will send in my name, will teach you [apostles] all things and will remind you of everything I have said to you . . .
>
> I have much more to say to you, more than you can now bear. But when he, the Spirit of truth, comes, he will guide you into all truth. He will not speak on his own; he will speak only what he hears, and he will tell you what is yet to come.
> (*Injil*, John 14:26; 16:12–13)

This gives us great confidence about John's Gospel and all the New Testament – God sent his Spirit to remind the apostles about Jesus and what the world needs to know about him. This provides further proof that the Counsellor cannot be Muhammad. Muhammad came 600 years later and could not remind the Eleven of anything.

The apostle Paul wrote something similar:

> All Scripture is God-breathed and is useful for teaching, rebuking, correcting and training in righteousness, so that the man of God may be thoroughly equipped for every good work.
> (*Injil*, 2 Timothy 3:16–17)

Here we are told that Scripture (which simply means 'writings' and is another way of saying 'the Bible') is breathed out by God. It is as if God breathes his words into people so that they can write these same words down. These words prepare people to live rightly and do good because they come from the good God who knows how we should live in his world.

The apostle Peter helps us to see this too:

> Above all, you must understand that no prophecy of
> Scripture came about by the prophet's own interpretation.
> For prophecy never had its origin in the will of man, but
> men spoke from God as they were carried along by the
> Holy Spirit.
> (*Injil*, 2 Peter 1:20–21)

The imagery here is of God blowing his prophets along like
a ship in the wind. God blows them along in the direction he
chooses. (This is made more apparent from the fact that the
word for 'Spirit' in Greek can also mean 'breath' or 'wind', a
play on words which Jesus also uses in John 3:5–8.) Therefore,
the words written down by the prophets and apostles appointed
by God didn't come from their own imagination, but from
God himself.

This can be hard to understand. How can something
be written by both God and human beings? Indeed, one
Muslim friend, Anwar, has quoted Surah 2:79 to me to
assert that this is another reason we cannot trust the Bible as
God's Word:

> Then woe to those who write the Book with their own hands,
> and then say 'This is from Allah.'

However, Yusuf Ali's footnotes to this verse and those sur-
rounding it make clear that only some Jews (not all Jews and
no Christians) are in view here and that they are accused of
making up bits of Scripture for personal gain.[8] It is not about
men taking up a pen and physically writing God's words down.
After all, the Qur'an was put down on paper by men's own
hands too.

God speaks to us through human words

The idea that the Bible is God speaking to us *through people* can still be a stumbling block to our Muslim friends. Part of this again goes back to their presuppositions – prophets and books come from God's dictation – but these assumptions are not based on how God has spoken in the past.

Almighty God has always revealed himself, his character and his plans to people through people. He has worked in and through their personalities, as well as in and through their culture. He has allowed people like Luke to carefully investigate all he has heard and then to write an orderly, historically accurate account of Jesus' life (Luke 1:1–4). God doesn't override the prophet or writer of Scripture, but rules over the author to make sure that what is written is from God. He blows the writers along through making them into the people he wants them to be and moving them to write the words he wants them to write.

In many ways, this is a very gracious act of God. God condescends to human language. He accommodates himself to people's limited communication and minds. God also accommodates himself in different styles.

Within the Bible's sixty-six books there is a variety of material and a range of writing styles. The Bible isn't limited to one type of literature because God wants it to speak into all different kinds of human experience. We have narrative, laws, ritual instructions, poetry, songs, sermons, prophecies, wisdom sayings, parables, letters and genealogies. This means that we can understand it using the normal human means of comprehending literary texts.

This 'human-ness' again confirms to us that we can translate the Bible. Its message is one we want all men and women to hear in their own heart-language or in a way they most clearly understand.[9]

Therefore, while the Bible was physically written by human beings, it consists of the true words of God and challenges people:

> For the word of God is living and active. Sharper than any double-edged sword, it penetrates even to dividing soul and spirit, joints and marrow; it judges the thoughts and attitudes of the heart. Nothing in all creation is hidden from God's sight. Everything is uncovered and laid bare before the eyes of him to whom we must give account.
> (*Injil*, Hebrews 4:12–13)

The Bible, as God's Word, is living just like God himself. It gives life, as Jesus said:

> The words I have spoken to you are spirit and they are life.
> (*Injil*, John 6:63)

It also reveals what we are like inside. It lays bare our hearts before God in our response to it. If we reject God's Word, we are rejecting God.

Therefore, in many ways, reading the Bible is a dangerous activity. It exposes what we are really like. Are we men and women who want to live under God's Word with soft hearts ready to do his will? Or will we harden our hearts, deceiving ourselves through our own sin, and so be unable to enter God's eternal paradise, the place of no crying or pain?

Some assurances from the Bible's content

The Bible understands people
In addition to its unified storyline and its God-breathed claims, we can also be sure that the Bible is from God's mind and not

people's own ideas because it understands and challenges every culture (as we saw in the last chapter). It also understands our world and its mess (as we have seen in the sections on sin and human hearts in previous chapters). It makes most sense of me and every other human.

For example, why are people capable of great acts of love and appalling acts of cruelty? Why can I praise someone one minute and in another minute curse somebody else, or even that same person I praised earlier if their back is turned? The answer is found in our creation and fall in Genesis 1 – 3, as we read that we are made in God's image yet we are flawed because of the corrupting effects of sin.

Other philosophies and religions do try to explain our world and can have helpful insights for us. To my mind, however, they don't seem to fit with the world we experience as closely as the Bible does. They don't adequately address the design of the world around us, the suffering we feel, the relationships we want to foster, the need for morality, the importance of government, the foundational aspect of marriage, what a human is, what happens after death, whether history has any meaning, how we can know what we know, why our world is full of diversity and unity – to name just a few issues. Every other worldview might have an answer to some of these issues, but not to all of them. (It would take another book to address each of these themes, but something like James Sire's *The Universe Next Door* [IVP, 2010] is a good place to begin.)

The Bible's God is unique

We also read about a personal God (as discussed in chapter 5) who cuts through individualism and totalitarianism. This God cannot be found in any other holy book. Again, this suggests that a human mind has not been capable of making up this concept of God. No religion has a Trinity, but every other

religion has either a version of monadic monotheism or polytheism. As C. S. Lewis said: 'If Christianity was something
we were making up, of course we would make it easier. But
it is not. We cannot compete, in simplicity, with people who
are inventing religions. How could we? We are dealing with
Fact. Of course, anyone can be simple if he has no facts to
bother about.'[10]

The Bible is full of fulfilled prophecies

Additionally, throughout the Bible there are examples of
prophecies being fulfilled. God says something will happen
and it does. Only God can know the future. Therefore, if
something in the future happens as the Bible says it will, this
again indicates that a Greater Mind is behind the Bible. Here
are just four examples, and there are many, many more:

- Abraham and Sarah had a son, Isaac (promised in
  Genesis 17:15–19 and fulfilled in Genesis 21:1–5).
- Israel was enslaved and rescued in Egypt (predicted in
  Genesis 15:13–16 and fulfilled in Exodus 12:40–41).
- God's righteous Servant suffered for other people's sins
  (promised in Isaiah 52:13 – 53:12 and fulfilled in Luke
  23:32–46).
- God's Anointed One/Messiah did not decay in the tomb
  (promised in Psalm 16:10 and fulfilled in Luke 24:45–47).

The Bible is authenticated by eyewitnesses

Just as prophecies authenticate the truth of the Bible's writings,
so there were people around at the time when the Bible was
written who could also authenticate these writings. For
example, when the people of Israel were rescued from Egypt
they came to Mount Sinai where God spoke to them. As the
prophet Moses recorded this event, the people who were with

him at Mount Sinai and read his words could confirm what he wrote. Moses' first readers saw and experienced the same things. The events were not seen just by one man up Mount Sinai. The people knew whether or not Moses was making them up. They were there too. God's actions and words were as real to them as they were to Moses.

Similarly, the events which the apostles wrote about were known by those around them. Many people saw Jesus the Messiah being crucified and over 500 people saw him alive after three days (1 Corinthians 15:3–8). These people could verify what the apostles wrote. It was not as if one apostle had gone off somewhere and come back with an idea which everyone then agreed with. Many people had seen and experienced exactly what the apostles had seen and experienced. They could vouch for its truth.

Indeed, the Gospel accounts are written in such a way as to encourage the original readers to ask these eyewitnesses about the events of Jesus' life. Therefore we are told about real people, such as: Jairus, a leader of the synagogue in Capernaum, whose daughter Jesus raised from the dead (Luke 8:41); Mary Magdalene, Joanna the wife of Chuza the manager of Herod's household, and Susanna who all followed Jesus as he taught the crowds, healed the sick and drove out demons (Luke 8:1–3); Simon from Cyrene who was forced to carry Jesus' cross and walk behind him on his way to be crucified (Luke 23:26); Joseph from Arimathea who helped to bury the dead Jesus (Luke 23:50–53); various named women, including Mary the mother of James, who first told the apostles about the empty tomb (24:9–11); and Cleopas who met the risen Jesus on the road to Emmaus (Luke 24:13–35).[11]

Why else would so many people be named in these Gospel accounts? Surely so that people could find them and ask them. These people were named so that, for example, anyone who read the Gospel accounts could go to Capernaum and ask Jairus what had happened to his daughter.

This also shows that the Gospel events must have been written in the lifetime of these people who met Jesus or else no-one would have been able to consult them. Just as there are people around today who can authenticate what happened on that first Bangladeshi Victory Day nearly forty years ago, so there were people around who could authenticate the accounts of Matthew, Mark, Luke and John. We have no reason for not taking their eyewitness testimony seriously.

The Qur'an and the previous Scriptures: part 2

I have suggested that we should view the Bible as a collection of books, written by men over time, to God's people, as inspired by the Holy Spirit (who created the writers, revealed the message to the prophets, ensured it was written down properly, and illumines believers to understand it rightly). Therefore it is God's word to humanity for all time. My Muslim friends often object to this because the Qur'an seems so different from the Bible. However, I would emphasize again that you cannot impose on the Bible the criteria for the Qur'anic revelation.

Some might say that there is no point reading the Bible because the Qur'an has superseded the Bible or because the Bible has been changed. However, the Qur'an says:

> Surely We have sent down the Torah wherein *are* guidance and light; thereby the prophets who had surrendered [to God] judge those of Jewry, by such of God's Book as they were ordained to observe and witness to. Hence, fear not the people, but fear Me, and sell not My signs for a paltry price. And whoever judges not by what God has sent down, then such are unbelievers.

And We decreed for them therein: life for life, and eye for eye, and nose for nose, and ear for ear, and tooth for tooth, and for wounds retaliation. But whoever forgoes it as a charity, that shall be an expiation for him. And whoever judges not by what God has sent down, such as they are the iniquitous.

And We have caused Jesus, son of Mary, to follow in their footsteps corroborating what was between his hands of the Torah, and We gave him the Gospel in which *is* guidance and light, confirming what he had between his hands of the Torah, as a guidance and an exhortation to the godfearing.

And let the people of the Evangel judge by what God has sent down therein, for whoever judges not by what God has sent down, then such as they are the miscreants.
(Surah 5:43–46)[12]

We can see that the Qur'an asserts that:

1. The Torah of the Old Testament is a revelation from God.
2. This Scripture is God's wisdom, guidance and light.
3. Jews are to judge according to their Scripture.
4. This Scripture in Muhammad's day was trustworthy.
5. The New Testament or 'Gospel' of Jesus is a revelation from God.
6. This Scripture is guidance and light from God.
7. Christians are to judge by God's revelation in their Scripture.
8. This Scripture in Muhammad's day was trustworthy.[13]

The Bible that we have in our hands is based on the same Hebrew and Greek texts which were around in Muhammad's day. Therefore the current Old and New Testaments are still guidance and light. Just focusing on the New Testament here, this means that there is guidance and light about the claims that Jesus is the ultimate fulfilment of God's promises (chapter 8) and that he truly died and rose again (chapter 3).

One Muslim friend, Said, kept telling me (usually over a good meal together, thankfully) how the Bible had been corrupted and was untrustworthy. I asked him how he accounted for these verses in his holy book. I am still waiting for an answer after two years.

Neither Said nor anyone else has ever produced a 'before and after' for the Bible to show where it has been changed. No documents, no people, no dates, no motives, no location for these changes have ever been shown to me. Indeed, most powerfully of all, both the Qur'an and the Bible tell us that God's Word cannot be changed.[14]

Life and protection from God's Word

Within certain forms of Islam, verses from the Qur'an are used to protect people from evil. Verses are sometimes written down on paper; the paper is then put in a cup of water so that the ink runs into the water and the person can drink in the Qur'an's protection. Other times, verses may be folded into tiny amulets to protect their wearers from the evil eye or demons or any form of misfortune.

The holy Bible is holy, but not in these ways. Its words come from God and so:

How sweet are your words to my taste,
sweeter than honey to my mouth!
I gain understanding from your precepts;
therefore I hate every wrong path.

Your word is a lamp to my feet
and a light for my path.

I have taken an oath and confirmed it,
>   that I will follow your righteous laws.
I have suffered much;
>   preserve my life, O Lord, according to your word.
(*Zabur*, Psalm 119:103–107)

We don't physically eat God's Word, but we do chew on it meditatively and enjoy its sweet refreshment of our souls. We do drink in its spiritual waters and so are guided in this life. Even in the face of suffering, it is God's Word which preserves us because it assures us of his never-ending love. God's Word is living and active in God's people.

I am amazed that no Muslim friend has ever offered to chew on the Qur'an with me. I realise that many think that the Qur'an can only be properly understood in Arabic and that there is less emphasis on comprehending than reciting. Yet my friends' devotion to the physical book – by reciting it or placing it on a top shelf or wearing an amulet filled with its verses – suggests that they don't believe that it has power to work in our souls. I long for them to read the Bible because I am convinced that God works in people through his Word. It is through God's Word that anyone can know God and be restored to him. Therefore his Word is to be read, meditated upon and put into practice.

Two very different Bengali men, one a university lecturer and the other an illegal immigrant working on the till of an Islamic bookshop, came to realize this. They looked at what the Qur'an says and found no evidence to believe that the Bible had been corrupted. Then they began to read the Bible with a follower of Jesus from a Muslim background. As Mahfuz and Zaid read God's story as revealed through prophets like Moses, they realized that the Bible did contain God's words and was his means of preserving their lives. Over a few months, as they meditated on God's promises and on the eyewitnesses confirming Jesus' claims to fulfil those promises, God's Spirit did his work through his Word and brought them to life and granted them forgiveness. They did not need Qur'anic amulets nor the polemic about corrupted texts. They had come to realize that God's Word was living and powerful in their own lives.

Key points

- The Bible is a collection of books, written by men over time, to God's people, as inspired by the Holy Spirit.
- It is God's living and powerful word to humanity for all time.
- There is no reason to believe that it has been corrupted or changed.

Some questions

For followers of Jesus the Messiah

- Why is it marvellous that God spoke through people to us in the Bible?
- In what ways are you tempted to doubt that the Bible is God's Word for all time?
- In what ways might these doubts hinder you from reading the Bible with unbelieving friends?

For Muslim friends

- What is stopping you from reading the Bible?
- Do you have as high a view of the Bible as the Qur'an does in Surah 5? Why/Why not?
- Would you be prepared to read Matthew's Gospel with a follower of Jesus?

8. How can we be sure about God?

Answers, assurance and hope

Good answers?
Just before Ramadan 2010, Sadiq texted me to say that his work had calmed down and we could again meet up for a 'religious chat'. We are at a similar age and stage in life so there was a lot of usual family stuff to catch up on. He had also been to university near where we live and there was a common local knowledge which brought us together. In previous 'religious chats' we had discussed sin, the Bible and how our respective faiths could solve our society's problems. I had always tried to talk about God in what I said, so that he could see how the Bible's description of God addressed these issues. However, we hadn't explicitly talked about either the Trinity or the incarnation and these were the issues he wanted to raise this time.

As we had our Prêt sandwiches on a bench outside my office, I did my best to outline who God is and how the Word could take on flesh. I had just finished drafts of chapters 4 and 5 of this book and was frantically trying to remember what I had written so that I could present something of a coherent argument. After each bit of explanation from me, a further question came from Sadiq. He was generally intrigued by what I was saying, but he was not convinced by my points. While he admitted that he could not tell me much about God because 'he is unknowable', he thought that my answers were not up to much.

Like many Muslim people who have the 'big four' objections mentioned in the introduction, Sadiq was not persuaded. You may be a Muslim person reading this chapter now, having been given this book by a Christian friend, and think similarly: *If that's the best these Christians can do in answering our questions, then I think I'll stick with Islam.* In my defence, I wouldn't dream of presuming that these are the best answers(!), but they are good ones inasmuch as they are based on the Scriptures as brought to us by God's prophets. More importantly than my defence, Sadiq and others show that God needs to be at work in any of us for us to change our minds on who he is.

The Holy Spirit is essential
Just as God's Holy Spirit was active in bringing the universe into existence, in enlivening dead bones in the prophet Ezekiel's day, in being necessary to enable entry into God's kingdom in the time of Jesus and his apostles,[1] so the Holy Spirit must be at work in people's lives now if they are to receive God's words. The apostle Paul knew this well:

. . . it is written:

No eye has seen,
no ear has heard,

no mind has conceived
  what God has prepared for those who love him
    [from Isaiah 64:4] –

but God has revealed it to us by his Spirit.
   The Spirit searches all things, even the deep things of God. For who among men knows the thoughts of a man except the man's spirit within him? In the same way no-one knows the thoughts of God except the Spirit of God. We have not received the spirit of the world but the Spirit who is from God, that we may understand what God has freely given us. This is what we speak, not in words taught us by human wisdom but in words taught by the Spirit, expressing spiritual truths in spiritual words. The man without the Spirit does not accept the things that come from the Spirit of God, for they are foolishness to him, and he cannot understand them, because they are spiritually discerned. (*Injil*, 1 Corinthians 2:9–14)

Reflecting such truths, Henry Martyn, a man who took the good news of Jesus to people in India and Persia, is quoted as saying, 'O that I could converse and reason, and plead, with power from on high. How powerless are the best-directed arguments, till the Holy Spirit renders them effectual.'[2] Therefore, if we want our Muslim friends to understand our biblical answers to their real questions, we must pray for the Holy Spirit to be at work. At the end of the day, it is God who draws people to himself. And if, as a Muslim reader, you genuinely want to understand these things of God, then ask for his Spirit to give you insight.

Central assurances

After discussing the nature of God for some time, Sadiq then said that he believed the Qur'an's testimony because it had come from an illiterate person, Muhammad. His argument was that Muhammad couldn't have made up such a wonderful book. It must have come from God himself. For example, Surah 7:157–158 says:

> Those who follow the Messenger, the unlettered Prophet, whom they find mentioned in their own (Scriptures), – in the Law and the Gospel; – for he commands them what is just and forbids them what is evil; he allows them as lawful what is good (and pure) and prohibits them from what is bad (and impure); He releases them from their heavy burdens and from the yokes that are upon them. So it is those who believe in him, honour him, help him, and follow the Light which is sent down with him, – it is they who will prosper.
>
> Say: 'O men! I am sent unto you all, as the Messenger of Allah, to Whom belongeth the dominion of the heavens and the earth: there is no god but He: it is He that giveth both life and death. So believe in God and His Messenger, the unlettered Prophet, who believeth in God and His words: follow him that (so) ye may be guided.'

Jesus the Messiah is the ultimate Prophet

Yusuf Ali's footnotes on these verses assert that 'the unlettered Prophet' means someone not versed in human learning and that this prophet mentioned 'in the Law and the Gospel' is Muhammad. Yusuf Ali argues, as do many other Muslim people, that the coming of Muhammad is prophesied in Deuteronomy 18:15 ('the Law') and in John 14:16 ('the Gospel'). However, there are numerous problems with this interpretation.

There is not enough space to go through all the difficulties, but a brief response is given here in order to both counter the misunderstanding and provide some profound reassurances

about the Christian message we have been looking at throughout this book.[3] First, Jesus was an untaught or unlettered
prophet. In John 7:14–24, the crowds and religious leaders
were astounded by Jesus' teaching because they knew that he
hadn't formally studied like the other rabbis. Throughout
the Gospel accounts, people were amazed when Jesus taught
them because he spoke with an authority which was lacking
from the other religious leaders. Even as a young boy he
impressed the rabbis and scribes of the Jerusalem temple with
his questions and understanding (Luke 2:46–48). The reason
for such untaught understanding was that Jesus the Messiah's
words came direct from the One who sent him.

Second, Muhammad cannot be the fulfilment of Deuteronomy 18 or John 14. I have already discussed John 14 in
chapter 7 on the Bible so I will just concentrate on Deuteronomy here. The prophet whom Moses looks forward to is
'from among your own brothers' (verse 15). This could
possibly be an Ishmaelite (Muhammad's distant ancestor) as
Isaac's half-brother. However, context is always crucial to
determine the meaning of words and in this instance
'brothers' is explained in an earlier verse. This section of
Deuteronomy also looks forward to the coming of a king
and Deuteronomy 17:15 says:

> . . . appoint over you the king the LORD your God chooses.
> He must be from among your own brothers. Do not place
> a foreigner over you, one who is not a brother Israelite.

'Brother' here means a fellow Israelite. Therefore, Israel's king
and prophet is to be a member of Israel.

Third, while Yusuf Ali's footnote points to Islam as a faith
that frees people from the restrictiveness of the Jewish religion
– Islam is 'a religion for freedom in the faith of Allah, of

universality in the variety of races, languages, manners and customs'[4] – I have argued earlier that Islam seems often tied to one culture and one time. It is, in fact, restrictive.

Islam is certainly more restrictive than Bible-centred Christianity. Yusuf Ali may well have recognized this as it is noticeable that he compares Islam with 'the exclusiveness of the Jews' rather than with the freedom of the Christians. Instead, as both Surah 3:50–51 and Matthew 15:1–20 state, Jesus the Messiah taught what is lawful, good and pure. Moreover, he also said (in beautiful words which Surah 7:157 echoes):

> Come to me, all you who are weary and burdened, and I will give you rest. Take my yoke upon you and learn from me, for I am gentle and humble in heart, and you will find rest for your souls. For my yoke is easy and my burden is light.
> (*Injil*, Matthew 11:28–30)

Jesus the Messiah releases people from the heavy labour of trying to achieve a righteous perfection. This is always out of our reach because we follow in Adam's footsteps of choosing to sin rather than trust in God. Instead, Jesus gives us his own perfect righteousness. He saw that people in his time were harassed and helpless because they were basically leaderless (Matthew 9:36). Their own teachers piled ever-increasing and unattainable burdens upon them because they were blind to any other way – it seemed that obeying rules was the way to please God (Matthew 23:1–4). Unlike these leaders, Jesus Christ is gentle and humble and has people's best interests at heart. He therefore came to give people the eternal rest and peace with God which they were made for and which Adam and Eve briefly enjoyed in the Garden before they sinned.

Jesus the Messiah is the ultimate one to serve

Taking Jesus' 'yoke' may sound like swapping one slavery for another, but in reality we all serve somebody (as even Bob Dylan famously sang). We are serving either ourselves or others and so the issue is whether we are serving what is best for us. Yes, Jesus demands our complete allegiance, but he is truly freeing because this is the way that we are supposed to live.

In terms of this brief book, Jesus' yoke means depending on the promises of the covenant-making God of the Bible (as discussed in chapter 1). It is serving others in our everyday life (chapter 2) as we become committed to other people. It is giving generously because we have been given so much. It is praying at all times because we want to talk to our Father, not because we have to. It is fasting privately so that only God knows what we're doing as we try to please him, not other people. It is walking in purity as we joyfully make our pilgrimage towards the new creation. It is being full of joy at being forgiven for our sins and having open access to our awesome Creator, thanks to our God who came to earth and sacrificed himself (chapters 3 and 4). It is following in the footsteps of the God who is three loving persons in perfect unity (chapter 5) and so living in relationship with other people as well as with our relational God. It takes seriously the human cultures that we looked at in chapter 6 and allows us to be at rest and enjoy the world God has placed us in, rather than withdrawing completely from it.

Jesus the Messiah is the ultimate fulfilment of God's plans

How can we know all this? How can we be assured of this wonderful rest and yoke? As we saw in chapter 7, the Bible should give us this confidence. Additionally, Matthew 11 is all about the certainty we can have concerning Jesus, as well as what he offers.

It begins with John the Baptist languishing in prison for daring to point out the sins of King Herod (who later beheaded him; see Matthew 14). From prison, John sent his disciples to ask Jesus if he was the one who had been promised, or whether someone else was going to come. John's issue seemed to be that his situation didn't fit with what he understood about God's Old Testament promises. After all, if he was in prison for following God, where was the rest and rescue which God's Messiah was supposed to bring?

Jesus replied:

> Go back and report to John what you hear and see: The blind receive sight, the lame walk, those who have leprosy are cured, the deaf hear, the dead are raised, and the good news is preached to the poor. Blessed is the man who does not fall away on account of me.
>
> (*Injil*, Matthew 11:4–6)

Jesus was the promised Rescuer because he was fulfilling the words of the prophets, such as Isaiah 35:4–6 and 61:1. As Matthew points out in his next chapter (Matthew 12:15–21), Jesus was the Servant promised in Isaiah 42:1–4 who was conquering sin and Satan at that time, and will bring full justice to the world when he returns. This means that John the Baptist was walking in the steps of Elijah (Matthew 11:14). He was fulfilling the words of the prophet Malachi who had said that Elijah would appear before the LORD God came to earth (Malachi 4:5).

So, for both John then and for us now, whether we are Christian or Muslim or anything else, the important thing is whether we will trust in this Messiah or fall away from him. Will we accept his teaching about himself on his terms? Or will we reject him because he doesn't fit our own preconceived ideas, as John was in danger of doing (but didn't!) and sadly as many Jewish people did in Jesus' own day.

Jesus is the ultimate Revealer of God

Fourth, returning to the issue of misunderstandings arising from Surah 7, Jesus Christ's teaching is not only 'light' in terms of weight, but also light in terms of revelation. Jesus is the Light which the Qur'an says was sent down. The prophet Isaiah promised that Light would dawn on 'Galilee of the Gentiles' as a Davidic, rescuing and everlasting king was born. The Light would open blind eyes among his own people Israel as well as people from other nations.[5] Jesus' life, his words and actions fit this prophecy.

Jesus Christ is the long-promised Prophet who speaks God's words and perfectly reveals him to us. He can do so because he is the Son who can alone reveal the Father (Matthew 11:25–27). This forms the ground on which he can certainly promise eternal rest (verses 28–29). Jesus graciously does so to people who are humble and childlike, not to those who sit over him in judgment (verses 20–26). It has to be an act of divine grace because as humans our sin naturally blinds us to this revelation. Just as Jesus opened the eyes of the physically blind, so he has to open the eyes of the spiritually blind.

Jesus the Messiah is the long-promised King who rescues his people from the dominion of sin, death and Satan. He is the one who guarantees life for his people now and for eternity. However tricky our Muslim friends' questions may be, however doubtful you as a Muslim may be of your Christian friends' answers, we can be certainly and joyfully assured that Jesus is the Light sent from God who can relieve all our burdens and bring us eternal rest. I haven't met a Muslim person who has such assurance from studying the Qur'an or following in Muhammad's footsteps.

Wider hope

Robert Bruce, a nineteenth-century missionary to Persia (present-day Iran-Iraq), is quoted as saying, 'I am not reaping the harvest; I can scarcely claim to be sowing the seed; I am hardly ploughing the soil; but I am gathering out the stones.'[6] As Bruce looked out on the harassed and helpless population of the Middle East – his harvest field – this was an honest assessment of the task before him. The many Muslim people around him seemed to be fairly resistant to the Christian gospel and to the kind of good answers and central assurances we have been looking at. I guess that he had met many Sadiqs.

As I look around my local area I see many, many Muslim people. There are probably well over 80,000 in our borough of 200,000 people. In London, the biggest student societies are usually the Islamic societies (the 'ISocs'). Within Britain, figures vary massively, but it is likely that there will be over 2.5 million Muslim people in the next census in 2011. Across the world there may be 1.4 billion Muslim people. That's a bigger harvest field than Robert Bruce probably imagined 200 years ago.

All of these people, whether in the Middle East, London or the university ISocs, are made in the image of God. Yet they are all fallen. They are all part of this beautiful world which God loves. Yet many seem so far from accepting the rest and the light yoke which are on offer from Jesus. However, this view of things misses at least two important details.

First, the Bible gives us real hope that many Muslim people will come to know the Lord Jesus. Abraham was promised that all peoples would be blessed through him and his offspring Jesus Christ (Genesis 12:1–3; Galatians 3:16). While this doesn't say that I can specifically expect Sadiq or Abdullah to be blessed by God and have their eyes opened by the Holy Spirit, I can have real confidence that members of their Muslim people-group will receive God's blessing.

Jesus tells us that he will build his church and that nothing will stand against it, least of all hell and all its forces opposed to God (Matthew 16:18). Therefore, just as certainly as he died and rose again in keeping with his words, so Jesus will build his gathering of worldwide believers. Nothing will prevent him from building his church in Asia, Africa or even London. I don't know whether Ruhana or Hasan themselves will be involved in this building project, but many members of their people-group will be.

The apostle John was given a vision of the future by the risen Lord Jesus and he reveals glimpses of it to us in the last book of the Bible. In Revelation 7:9–12 we are told that 'a great multitude that no-one could count, from every nation, tribe, people and language' is around the Lord Jesus praising him for all eternity. I don't know whether Asad or Hussein will be in this great multitude, but I know that people from their language group will be there praising God in their native tongues.

Second, history shows that God's Holy Spirit is steadily opening the eyes of Muslim people to see who Jesus is. Robert Bruce gathered out some stones. Those who followed him ploughed the soil and sowed some seed. Now there are tens of thousands of Iranian believers from Muslim backgrounds both within the country and within the Iranian diaspora around the world. It is exciting to realize that more Iranians from a Muslim background have come to believe in Jesus since the 1979 Revolution than in the previous 2,000 years.[7]

Across the world many Muslim people are finally getting the chance to have ongoing exposure to God's Word and have their objections answered lovingly by Christian people. While it is a long and slow process at times, people from many

Muslim people-groups are beginning to turn to Jesus, from Morocco in the west to Indonesia in the east. Indeed, although there were only a handful of believers from a Muslim background in the UK thirty years ago, there are now conferences specifically for new believers who have recently left Islam.

This analysis of the current situation isn't meant to make us feel proud or to show off ('my church is bigger than your mosque'), but just to remind Jesus' followers that God is quietly working. It is also to help our Muslim friends see that 'Ubaydullah in chapter 1, Ishaq in chapter 3, Yahya in chapter 4 and Mahfuz and Zaid in chapter 7 are not the only people from Muslim backgrounds who have stopped blinking and have seen the light. My prayer is that God the Holy Spirit will open many more eyes and hearts to see the wonders of Jesus Christ and therefore know a life of joy with our heavenly Father.

Key points

- Jesus the Messiah is the ultimate Light who reveals God to us and brings us rest from our burdens.
- Only God the Holy Spirit can reveal this truth to us.
- God is doing this work among Muslim people as his Word goes out across the world.

Some questions

For followers of Jesus the Messiah

- What are all the blessings which Jesus brings to those who believe in him? Take time to rejoice in them now.
- Why not pray that you will have an opportunity to share these blessings with a Muslim friend? Take time to pray now.

- Why not commit to praying for a particular Muslim people-group to begin following Jesus?[8]

For Muslim friends

- What assurance of eternal rest does your religion give you?
- What certain and personal knowledge of God does your religion give you?
- What is stopping you from accepting Jesus the Messiah's offer of rest and service?

Notes

Introduction: Questions, objections and confusion

1. The name has been changed, as have all names of Christian or Muslim friends in this book.

2. For example, one group of Muslim scholars, called the Mu'tazilites thought that the Qur'an must be created because there is only one eternal being and that is God. An eternal, uncreated Qur'an would be a rival to him.

3. Within the Qur'an there is a recognition that God gave books to particular prophets, such as the *Taurat* or Pentateuch to Moses, the *Zabur* or Psalms to David, and the *Injil* or New Testament to Jesus. Every so often, I have used these terms alongside Bible ones so that our Muslim friends will understand where we are basing our thoughts.

4. Some Muslim people would not include the sixth as central. However, every Muslim I have met would agree with six beliefs. The same is true of popular literature such as I. A. Abu-Harb, *A Brief Illustrated Guide to Understanding Islam* (Darussalam, 1997), which is often given out by mosques and Islamic societies in London, and websites such as http://en. wikipedia.org/wiki/Islam. Both the five pillars and six beliefs can be discerned from the Qur'an, but they are summarized in this way by Muhammad according to Ibn Umar, one of the earliest followers of Muhammad, in Sahih Al-Bukhari, Hadith no. 8 and quoted in appendix II of *The Noble Qur'an in the English Language* translated by Khan and Al-Hilali.

5. This book focuses on these kinds of objections, rather than historical or cultural barriers to believing the Christian message. A great resource for thinking through these other barriers is Steve Bell's *Friendship First: The Manual* (Friendship First Publications, 2003).

6. The important thing is to see whether our doctrine agrees with what the Bible teaches and that we sit under holy Scripture's authority rather than stand over it and refuse to respond to its doctrine.

7. Bill Musk's *The Unseen Face of Islam* (Monarch, 2003) is really helpful in understanding this. The next paragraph is a massive oversimplification of chapters 13 to 14 from his book.

8. Such as the creeds of Nicea and Chalcedon, the Church of England's Thirty-Nine Articles and the Westminster Confession, and the Evangelical Alliance's Statement of Faith and the Chicago Statement on Biblical Inerrancy.

9. See James 2:23; Galatians 3:6 – 4:31.

Chapter 1 How can we know an incomprehensible God?

1. Unless otherwise stated, all Bible references are from the New International Version. For more information on Bible translations, please see chapter 7's discussion of 'language'.

2. It is clear that Moses could not have written all of the first five biblical books, such as Deuteronomy 34:10–12. However, Jesus himself refers to Moses as their author; for example in Matthew 19:1–8 and Mark 12:26. A helpful book on Jesus' view of the Old Testament is John Wenham, *Christ and the Bible* (Baker Book House, 1984).

3. Adm. by worshiptogether.com songs excl. UK & Europe, adm. by kingswaysongs.com tym@kingsway.co.uk. Used by permission.

4. The word 'LORD' in capitals is an English rendering of the divine name YHWH (Yahweh or Jehovah) which was first revealed to the prophet Moses in Exodus 3:14.

5. See for example Deuteronomy 4:1–40; 1 Kings 18; Exodus
   7 – 12; Isaiah 40 – 41 respectively.
6. See for example the prophet Hosea.
7. Ibn Ishaq, *The Life of Muhammad*, translated by A. Guillaume
   (OUP, 2001), p. 99, paragraphs 143–144.

Chapter 2 Don't Christians only do Sundays?

1. See 'How Christianity Conquered Rome' at http://www.
   perryville.org/?p=523 for more details or Rodney Stark,
   *Cities of God: The Real Story of How Christianity Became an
   Urban Movement and Conquered Rome* (HarperOne, 2006),
   p. 31.
2. See also D. A. Carson, *Christ and Culture Revisited* (Apollos,
   2008), pp. 56–58.
3. Wayne Grudem points out that 'God is often pleased to give
   honour to those who are weaker or less honoured in the
   eyes of the world (*cf.* Mt. 5:3–12; 1 Cor 1:26–30; 12:22–25;
   Jas. 2:5; 4:6; 1 Pet 5:5) . . . Peter does not specify the way in
   which he understands the woman to be *the weaker sex*, but
   the context would make it appropriate for him to have in
   mind any kind of weakness of which husbands would need
   to be cautioned not to take advantage.' Wayne Grudem,
   1 Peter, Tyndale New Testament Commentaries (IVP, 1988),
   pp. 143–144.
4. See Grudem, *1 Peter*, on these verses for more detail and an
   engagement with alternative Christian views.
5. From Piper's sermon, online at http://www.desiringgod.
   org/ResourceLibrary/Sermons/ByScripture/4/881_
   Women_of_Valor_for_NonPromise_Keepers. Copyright
   1994 John Piper. Used by permission (www.desiringgod.org).
6. See, for example, Solomon's Proverbs 23:10–11; 1:8 – 9:18.
7. These actions can be gleaned from Scripture. For example,
   1 Corinthians 6:18; Proverbs 16:28; Luke 12:15 for the 'do
   nots' and Proverbs 25:25; 1 Timothy 6:18; Matthew 28:18–20
   for the 'dos' respectively.

Chapter 3 What sort of God can be murdered?

1. Friedrich Nietzsche, *The Gay Science* (1882, 1887), paragraph 125, ed. Walter Kaufmann (Vintage, 1974), p. 181.

2. You can view an online copy at http://www.jamaat.net/ crux/crucifixion.html.

3. For more on this, see, for example, Garry Williams, *The Da Vinci Code: From Dan Brown's Fiction to Mary Magdalene's Faith* (Christian Focus, 2006); John Dickson, *The Christ Files: How Historians Know What They Know About Jesus* (Blue Bottle Books, 2006); Rodney Stark, *Cities of God: The Real Story of How Christianity Became an Urban Movement and Conquered Rome* (HarperOne, 2006), especially chapters 6 and 7.

4. The word 'qurbaan' (قُرْبان) comes from the Arabic root 'q r b' (ق ر ب). The most basic form of the root is the verb 'qaruba' (قَرُبَ) which means 'to come near, to get close, to close in, to approach. The noun derived from the primary verb is 'qurb' (قُرْب) meaning 'closeness, proximity, nearness'. The noun 'qurbaa'(قُرْبى) means 'relationship or kinship'. There is also another noun 'qurba' (قُرْبة) which means 'an act pleasing to God'. These references can be found in 'The Hans Wehr Dictionary of Modern Written Arabic', 4th Edition, Ed. J. M. Cowan, Spoken Language services Inc., Urbana IL, 1994, pp. 882–884. This is the best Arabic English dictionary, and the one recommended on university Arabic courses. I am grateful to Richard G-S for finding this for me.

5. For example, Yusuf Ali's footnotes 4098–4102 in *The Meaning of the Holy Qur'an*, eleventh edition (Amana Publications, 2008), promote this interpretation.

6. Yusuf Ali, *The Meanings of the Holy Qur'an* (Islamic Book Service, 2000), footnote 17. Please note that this is a different edition from the one used previously.

7. If this really is an issue for you and you cannot believe in the crucifixion without understanding this first, then please read Steve Jeffery, Mike Ovey and Andrew Sach, *Pierced for Our Transgressions* (IVP, 2007), pp. 247–248.

8. Some people do not see the Psalms as prophetic. However, as Derek Kidner points out, 'No incident recorded of David can begin to account for this.' Rather, '"Being therefore a prophet . . . he foresaw and spoke of . . . the Christ" (Acts 2:30f.).' See his *Psalms 1 – 72*, Tyndale Old Testament Commentaries (IVP, 1973), p. 105.

9. In *Al-Tafsir al-Kabir*, IV:8, pp. 62–63; summarized in Chawcat Moucarry, *Faith to Faith* (IVP, 2001), pp. 134–137.

Chapter 4 What sort of God can be born as a baby?

1. Yusuf Ali, *The Meaning of the Holy Qur'an*, eleventh edition (Amana Publications, 2008), footnote 6299.

2. As D. A. Carson points out in his commentary *The Gospel According to John* (Apollos, 1991), p. 129: 'The italicized words spell out the nature of that goodness which is God's glory. The two crucial words in Hebrew are *hesed* (variously rendered "steadfast love", "mercy", "covenant love" – but it has recently been shown quite clearly that it is the *graciousness* of love that is at stake) and '*met* ("truth" or "faithfulness").'

3. See John 4:26; 6:20; 8:24, 28, 58; 13:19; 18:5, 6, 8; compare Deuteronomy 32:39; Isaiah 41:4; 43:10, 11, 13, 25; 46:4; 51:12; 52:6 as Richard Bauckham points out in the reprint of his book *God Crucified* as a chapter of *Jesus and the God of Israel* (Paternoster Press, 2008), p. 40.

4. For example, in Surah 72:3 and Yusuf Ali, *The Meaning of the Holy Qur'an*, eleventh edition (Amana Publications, 2008), footnotes 5727, 5730.

5. This is the title of chapter 2 of Athanasius' work *On the Incarnation*, section 6, accessible at http://www.ccel.org/ccel/athanasius/incarnation.iii.html; this section seeks to summarize his argument.

6. No, this is not a typo for 'vice-regents'! A vice-regent is someone who rules on behalf of another who cannot rule due to being absent, or ill, or too young. A vice-regent is a substitute. This is obviously not true for human beings and

God. God is always the present, powerful and eternal Creator and human beings are not his substitute.

7. Athanasius, *On the Incarnation*, chapter 2, section 8, accessible at http://www.ccel.org/ccel/athanasius/incarnation.iii.html.

8. Athanasius, *On the Incarnation*, chapter 2, section 9, accessible at http://www.ccel.org/ccel/athanasius/incarnation.iii.html. I am grateful to Andrew Sach for showing me this particular quote.

9. See a summary of the teaching of Irenaeus on this at http://www.theopedia.com/Irenaeus.

10. Surah 2:116 has been translated variously as 'They say: "God has taken/adopted/begotten a son."' See also Surah 19:35. The ninth-century Christian theologian Abu Ra'ita in Baghdad plays on 'take son' and 'take flesh' in his apologetic for Muslim people. See Mark Beaumont, *Christology in Dialogue with Muslims* (Paternoster, 2005), pp. 44–66.

Chapter 5 But don't Christians worship three Gods?

1. Gregory of Nyssa (born c. 385) addressed this very issue in 'On not three gods', online at http://www.newadvent.org/fathers/2905.htm.

2. I am grateful for Mike Ovey's help in seeing this more clearly through his Oak Hill doctrine lectures.

3. It is also tempting to say that the one Arsenal is made up of more than one person, so that there are many persons acting unitedly in the one being that is Arsenal, but it might be best to leave footballing analogies and the Trinity there for now!

4. It is interesting that just after affirming the oneness of God, Jesus quotes Psalm 110 (in Mark 12:35–37) to expand people's view of God.

5. Just as the Word of Allah (the Qur'an) seems to be eternal and distinct from Allah. Within a century of the death of Muhammad, Muslim people were actively wrestling with the

existence of two eternal beings – Allah and the Word of Allah – as the Mu'tazilites' controversy showed.

6. I am grateful to Mike Ovey for showing this to me.

7. See for example http://www.islam.tc/beard/beard.html for an orthodox website on this.

8. This is not the position of all Muslim people and there are some commendable moves to overturn the apostasy laws (see Sheikh Tantawi's views [the previous Grand Imam of Al-Azhar University in Cairo] at http://www.sunnah.org/history/Scholars/mashaykh_azhar.htm. He says that an apostate should be left alone as long as he or she does not pose a threat to Islam). However, this is the position of the four orthodox schools of Islamic jurisprudence. This is based on *hadith* such as Bukhari, vol. 9, no. 17: 'Narrated Abdullah: Allah's Messenger said, "The blood of a Muslim who confesses that none has the right to be worshipped but Allah and that I am His Messenger, cannot be shed except in three cases: in Qisas (equality in punishment) for murder, a married person who commits illegal sexual intercourse and the one who reverts from Islam (Apostate) and leaves the Muslims."' (See also Bukhari, vol. 9, nos 57, 58.) Both Muslim and Christian websites contain more on this: http://muslim-canada.org/apostasy.htm and http://www.answering-islam.org/Silas/apostasy.htm.

9. We see this community now in the church and ultimately in the new creation, in places like Ephesians 2 and Revelation 7, but there is not space to develop this further here. One good book on this is Christopher Ash, *Remaking a Broken World* (Authentic Media, 2010).

10. Maurice Godelier, *The Mental and the Material* (Verso, 1986) p. 1; quoted in Michael Carrithers, *Why Humans Have Cultures: Explaining Anthropology and Social Diversity* (OUP, 1992), p. 1.

11. Steve Bell, *Gospel for Muslims: An Eastern Telling of the Good News about Jesus* (Authentic Media, 2011). Illustration given

by Bernie Powers of Interserve Australia. I am grateful to Steve Bell for allowing me permission to use this prior to publication.

Chapter 6 Where does Christianity end and Western culture begin?

1. Tim Keller of Redeemer Church in New York develops this idea further in various lectures he has given at church planting conferences in London.

2. I guess the real shame is that we have so many versions/ translations in English, when 300 million people across the world do not have God's good news in their own language. See http://wycliffe.org.uk/ for further information.

3. John Richardson, *What God Has Made Clean: If We Can Eat Prawns, Why Is Gay Sex Wrong?* (MPA Books/The Good Book Company, 2003) makes a similar point in pp. 12–13.

4. Passages like Matthew 5:17–20; Romans 6 – 7; Galatians 3:23 – 4:7 and Ephesians 2:11–22 are all helpful in this regard.

5. See for example 1 Corinthians 6:9–20; 10:32; 1 Peter 3:3–4.

6. See for example 1 Corinthians 7:19; Galatians 5:6; 6:15.

Chapter 7 Hasn't the Bible been corrupted?

1. Yusuf Ali, *The Meaning of the Holy Qur'an*, eleventh edition (Amana Publications 2008), footnotes 565, 746.

2. Ibn Kathir was born in 701 and one of his students, Ibn Hajji, described him: 'He had the best memory of the Hadith texts. He also had the most knowledge concerning the narrators and authenticity, his contemporaries and teachers admitted to these qualities. Every time I met him I gained some benefit from him.' A compilation of *The Abridged Tafsir Ibn Kathir Volumes 1 – 10: In the English Language with Arabic Verses* can be found at http://www.abdurrahman.org/qurantafseer/ ibnkathir/ along with his biographical details.

3. From http://ibnkathir.atspace.com/ibnkathir/ibnkathir_web/5.13875.html.

4. Colin Chapman's *Cross and Crescent* (IVP, 2002), pp. 186–188, provides some helpful background here.

5. *Desh* means country in Bengali and *Bangla* is what the Bengali language is called by its native speakers.

6. It was on 16 December 1971, as India's Army helped the Bangladesh Liberation Army against (West) Pakistan.

7. Another Bible verse that Muslim friends often use to say that Muhammad is promised is in Deuteronomy 18. This is dealt with in chapter 8.

8. Ali, *Meaning of the Holy Qur'an*, footnote 84.

9. See chapter 7's discussion of 'language' for more on Bible translations.

10. C. S. Lewis, *Mere Christianity* (Fount, 1977), p. 141.

11. See Richard Bauckham, *Jesus and the Eyewitnesses: The Gospels as Eyewitness Testimony* (Eerdmans, 2006) for more information.

12. M. M. Khatib's *Translation of the Qur'an*, which is authorized by Al-Azhar University (the most authoritative seat of Sunni learning), my italics. I have not used Yusuf Ali's translation here because he has mistranslated the emphasized verbs, turning them into perfect tenses rather than present tenses; for example, there *was* guidance and light in the *Taurat* and *Injil*. This makes a mockery of some Muslim people's accusations that Bible translations are based on the translators' own biases.

13. I am grateful to Martinez Vestibule for showing me this as part of a seminar he organized.

14. See for example Surah 10:64; Numbers 23:18–20; Isaiah 40:6–8. Bart Ehrman's books, such as *Misquoting Jesus* (Harper, 2005), are often used by all kinds of people to assert that the Scriptures have been changed. However, Ehrman's position is comprehensively critiqued and debunked in Andreas J. Köstenberger and Michael J. Kruger, *The Heresy of Orthodoxy* (Apollos, 2010).

Chapter 8 How can we be sure about God?

1. See for example Genesis 1:2; Ezekiel 37; John 3:1–8; Acts 2.
2. Henry Martyn, *Journals and Letters of Henry Martyn*, vol. 2, ed. S. Wilberforce (Seely and Burnside, 1837), p. 373; quoted in Colin Chapman, *Cross and Crescent* (IVP, 1995), p. 172.
3. One difficulty I do not address is that 'unlettered' is itself a bad translation of the Arabic word *ummiyun*. It could mean 'of the Gentiles'. See Jeremy Hinds' *Course on the Qur'an*, p. 39: 'For "umma" means "people" and the plural indicates "tribes" or in the Biblical idiom "Gentiles."' This could, therefore, echo Isaiah 42:5–9 and 49:5–6 and point to Jesus. However, rather than dispute the translation, I am going with Yusuf Ali's understanding, but will push that in a Christian direction.
4. Yusuf Ali, *The Meaning of the Holy Qur'an*, eleventh edition (Amana Publications, 2008), footnote 1128.
5. See Isaiah 9:1–7; 42:6–7; 49:5–6.
6. Quoted from *History of the Church Missionary Society*, vol. iii (Eugene Stock, 1899), p. 125, in Colin Chapman, *Cross and Crescent* (IVP, 1995), p. 14.
7. Believers in Iran are conservatively estimated at 100,000. Whatever the figure, the vast majority are from a Muslim background. Both the scattering of the Iranian people across the world and their gradual restoration to God seem to be a fulfilment of God's promises at the end of Jeremiah 49:34–39. The following websites contain some helpful information on the church in Iran and I am grateful to Linguist Dan for pointing me here: http://www.elam.com/articles/Church-in-Iran/ and http://www.30–days.net/muslims/muslims-in/mid-near-east/iran-insights.
8. Good resources for prayer can be found at http://www.30-days.net.